TEAM
CHAMPION!

SUcMPCwPSN

UcMPCwPSN/-1 of 1-/std-uk-dom/0 A1

Thank
you for
shopping
at
Amazon.co.uk!

Packing slip for

Your order of 15 November 2021
Order ID 206-6573881-5837148

Packing slip number UcMPCwPSN
Shipping date 15 November 2021

Qty.	Order Summary	Bin
1	Team Champion!: Taking Teamwork Seriously Paperback, Allan Mackintosh, 1800463731 : 1800463731: 9791800463738	

This shipment completes your order.

You can always check the status of your orders or change your account details from the "Your Account" link at the top of each page on our site

Thinking of returning an item? PLEASE USE OUR ON-LINE RETURNS SUPPORT CENTRE.

Our Returns Support Centre (www.amazon.co.uk/returns-support) will guide you through our Returns
Policy and provide you with a printable personalised return label. Please have your order number ready (you
can find it next to your order summary, above). Our Returns Policy does not affect your statutory rights

0/UcMPCwPSN/-1 of 1-//AMZL-DBIS-ND/std-uk-dom/0/1116-17:30/1116-03:54 Pack Type : A1

TEAM CHAMPION!

Taking Teamwork Seriously

A Straight-Talking Guide to Creating,
Sustaining and Unlocking the Potential
of High-Performance Teams.

ALLAN MACKINTOSH

Matador
9 Priory Business Park,
Wistow Road, Kibworth Beauchamp,
Leicestershire. LE8 0RX
Tel: 0116 279 2299
Email: books@troubador.co.uk
Web: www.troubador.co.uk/matador
Twitter: @matadorbooks

ISBN 978 1800463 738

British Library Cataloguing in Publication Data.
A catalogue record for this book is available from the British Library.

Printed and bound by CPI Group (UK) Ltd, Croydon, CR0 4YY
Typeset in 11pt Gill Sans MT by Troubador Publishing Ltd, Leicester, UK

Matador is an imprint of Troubador Publishing Ltd

Acknowledgements

In my first book, *The Successful Coaching Manager* (Troubador Press, 2003), I was indebted to my family, which comprises my wife, Shirley, son, Kerr and daughter, Heather. Both Kerr and Heather are away from home now, having graduated from University and in full employment. However, they still provided encouragement from afar and in some instances much needed IT assistance! My wife, Shirley, once again provided invaluable encouragement and inspiration in relation to my being disciplined and taking the time to sit down and write!

To my former work colleagues and the many network contacts I have made over the years, I would also like to thank them for their words of encouragement as well as sharing their experiences of teams, both in business and in the sports arena.

They are too numerous to mention, but they know who they are!

I am also indebted to Trudy Bateman and the Leadership Team of the University of Glasgow's Men's Rugby Club. Trudy provided the chapter on Strengths. Without Trudy's unrivalled expertise in the area of personal Strengths and Strength Profiling, I would have found this chapter particularly challenging as it's not one of my Strengths! The Leadership Team of Men's Rugby at the University of Glasgow have allowed me to share a key element of their team contract which allows the reader to get a 'feel' for what a team contract may look like, so a big thank you to them also.

Preface

This book is for all team managers, team supervisors, team leaders and all those who aspire to lead teams in the future. It is also aimed at ordinary team members, who, when they are more informed and knowledgeable about essential team processes and team dynamics, will be able to assist and support their team managers, supervisors, and leaders to move the team to high performance – and to stay there.

I have tried to ensure that this book, is easy to read, easy to understand and reflects the reader's own individual experiences. Above all I hope the contents of the book will inspire the reader to act and to utilise their newly found knowledge of teams with the business or sports teams that they lead or are simply a member of.

In addition, I have kept the theory to a minimum and have outlined the key theories that I know work in practice when applied effectively and consistently. I have also deliberately kept the book relatively short in comparison to many business books, as I know from experience that many team managers, team supervisors, and team leaders prefer business books to be kept brief, succinct and action centred.

Above all, I hope that you find the book and its contents informative and illuminating and that it will go a long way to ensuring that your leadership or membership of teams is both productive and motivational.

Yours Aye,
Allan Mackintosh

Team Champion, Coach, Speaker & Author.
Partners Team Development.
www.partnersteamdevelopment.com

Introduction

It was a cold, damp, and grey Saturday morning in November 1972. As I stood admiring the list of Scotland Rugby internationalists whose names were remembered in gold leaf on the beautifully varnished boards hung in the wonderful old sports pavilion at The High School of Glasgow, Old Anniesland, Glasgow, I felt a tap on my shoulder. "Well played today, Mackintosh. You led by example. Maybe one day your name will be up there". I felt a burst of pride. I had played one of my better games of rugby for Marr College's 1st Year A team against our High School of Glasgow counterparts and my last-minute penalty had secured us a 17-17 draw and a moral victory in the 'comprehensive, state school' versus 'independent, private school' battle. The tap on the shoulder was from our Junior School rugby coach, the legendary 'Papa Hardie' who remains to this day one of the best motivators that I have encountered. As an aside, I did get my name on one of these immaculately varnished boards some thirty-five years later, but not as a player, only as the Chairman of the Scottish Premiership rugby side, Glasgow Hawks. A bad knee injury sustained whilst training with my then club side, Glasgow High Kelvinside, ironically at Old Anniesland, when I was twenty-four, put paid to any top-class rugby career. Well, that is my story, and I am sticking to it!

At the end of my first season of playing secondary school rugby at Marr (no mini rugby in those days), I was a total convert to the game and as we had played well as a team that season (albeit, relying on several 'bigger' lads who had reached puberty quicker than most of us!) I was looking forward to moving into 2nd Year and the next season could not come quick enough. At the final training session, I was approached by 'Papa' Hardie, and told that, in conjunction with the other coaches, they had decided that I would be captain of the 2nd Year 'A' Team for the forthcoming season. I was over the moon and skipped all the way home to announce to my father (who was a handy player in his day with Glasgow University) that I had been made captain. "Well done and well deserved" he said, "now you'll learn all about team leadership." I was to learn very quickly how true these words were!

When the season started and we were all back at school after the summer break, I quickly noticed how a good number of the rugby players in my year had changed physically and mentally. Some had grown taller but not put any weight on; some had not grown-up height-wise but were wider and more round; a few had not grown at all and looked very slight, and there were a good few who seemed to have developed a 'rebel' attitude that seemed to enable them to challenge anything that was said, although no one 'challenged' Papa Hardie! When the teams were selected, my 'A' Team bore little resemblance to the previous year's team, both in terms of personnel and in physical presence! My mates were now in the 'B' Team and I was now the captain of what I would only describe as a collection of misfits and rebels. This is when it started to go wrong for me as a team captain.

My previous experience of team captaincy was only that of being 'captained' and this was limited to my later years of primary school football and one year of rugby at secondary school. My previous captains would shout, moan, blame and generally 'bully' their way through matches. You ignored them as best you could and got on with your game. The motivation would come from the touchlines through the coaches and if the truth be told, the only motivator was old 'Papa', as many of the parents were not exactly motivational given that they could not see beyond their own child. So, when I started out as team captain, I did what only I knew best, and shouted at my fellow players although I was careful not to 'point the finger of blame' as my father had drummed into me that blaming people was not a great trait and that you should always look to encourage people even when they make mistakes. However, this 'captaining' lark was tough and with the 'bigger' lads not liking being shouted at (even though I thought I was encouraging them!) I soon found myself being shunned as the team captain. My game went to pieces and even the constant support from 'Papa' Hardie was not enough to stop me becoming disillusioned with captaincy and indeed the game of rugby itself. I was learning a harsh lesson about team captaincy and about teams in general. As a result of my game deteriorating, I was dropped into the 'B' Team and told to concentrate on getting my enjoyment for the game back.

I continued to play rugby at secondary school, but I never took it seriously again until my final years when a chance to get into the 1st XV appeared. I took it and played in an excellent 1st XV where there was a lot more emphasis on teamwork, game plans and skills development. This felt a lot better! There was a winning attitude, a good level of rapport between the squad members (with a high level of skill and support) and there was an excellent level of support and encouragement from the coaches. And to cap it all, it was a winning team. Maybe teams were not such a bad place to be after all.

From secondary school I went on to play senior rugby and when playing for Glasgow University I was made Captain of Men's Rugby in my third year in 1980. Whilst the desire to go for captain was strong there was a nervousness still lingering from my early secondary school experience. Although I enjoyed my year of captaincy at University in a very mixed season in terms of success, it was still a challenging year as I was very conscious that team captaincy still appeared to be a very lonely place with an expectation of leading by example both on and off the field. It was during this year that I started to look into broadening my knowledge of team dynamics and high-performance teams and the more I read, the more I realised that teams are extraordinarily complex organisms, and that they need a lot of care and attention in order to make them work effectively and indeed thrive. If I knew then, back in 1980, what I now know, then my approach to captaining the University 1st XV would have been a lot different! And perhaps the results would have been a lot better also!

From these early sporting experiences in teams, I went into business and quickly learned that business in general knows even less about teams and team dynamics than sports teams do. Despite there being a mass of published theory around business teams, the challenge is that many organisations simply pay 'lip service' to the theory of teams and the practical application of even the basics of team performance and development. There is an expectation from senior leadership that managers know all about the basics of teams and can immediately get a team up and running to high performance. I know this to be far from the truth and that the key focus of most managers is to get the team up and running by diving straight into task. This results only in mediocre performance at best and if only more attention is given to the basics of team performance then greater results will ultimately follow with the full potential of the team being realised.

This book is dedicated to enabling team managers and leaders to learn the basics of team development and to put these basics into practical application. I make no apology for concentrating on the basics because if managers and team leaders can get these basics right then it will stand them, and their teams, in good stead to go on and go through the various stages of team development to becoming a high-performance team.

"The disciplined application of "team basics" is often overlooked. Team basics include size, purpose, goals, skills, approach, and accountability. Paying rigorous attention to these is what creates the conditions necessary for team performance. A deficiency in any of these areas will derail the team, yet most potential teams inadvertently ignore one or more of them"

"The Wisdom of Teams" by Jon R Katzenbach & Douglas K Smith.

Contents

Are Teams & Teamwork Being Taken Seriously?

There is a lot of discussion around present events (this is being written during the 2020-21 COVID-19 pandemic) and the fact that businesses will have to change the way they work in the future. There is also a lot of debate about moving to more remote and virtual team working and with many workforces 'off the road' or 'out of the office' just now, this move to remote team working is already happening. In fact, this change has been happening for a while now and this move to more remote team working is only being accelerated by the COVID-19 pandemic. So where does this place the future of work-related teams?

It is generally accepted that teams are vital to the productivity of business and are needed to gain competitive advantage whether they be physical 'workplace' teams, 'geographically separated' sales and project teams or global 'virtual' project teams. Despite the present pandemic the vital importance of high-performance teams will not diminish — in fact with the potential for companies to downsize due to

COVID-19 then the importance of creating and sustaining high performance teams will most definitely increase. And this will happen both in remote and virtual teams as well as workplace teams where they meet physically. So why is team development not on every organisation capability plan and why is so little done to continually develop the skills of team leadership in team managers and leaders? Now, I expect some of you reading this to highlight that most management leadership courses do provide information and instruction on how to lead teams effectively. And, yes, I would agree that there are masses of courses, books, blogs, articles, and videos out there that highlight what is needed for organisations, managers, and team leaders to learn more about high performance teams and how to lead them effectively. However, my questions are around just how much is really done to ensure that the learning from these resources is effectively put into practice and sustained? How many organisations have 'Teamwork' as a key company value but in effect do little, if anything, to properly develop team managers and project leaders in how to create and lead high performance teams? How many organisations have team development capability detailed in their company capability or training plan? How many team managers and team leaders really know the essential basics of teams in terms of the developmental models that need to be applied to guide the team from creation to high performance? How many organisations have invested in team coaches?

My experience is unfortunately that a good number of organisations I have knowledge of do not take teamwork as seriously as they should. They have 'teamwork' as one of their values, have it emblazoned on office walls, posters and employee materials but then pass on responsibility for developing the skills of teamwork to the managers and team leaders themselves, under the guise of 'self-development',, citing that the organisation's view is that the responsibility for learning sits with the employee. I am all for 'self-learning' and being 'responsible' but there must be some situations where the organisation actually takes the lead and provides resources and events to enable their team managers and project leaders to properly develop the skills and knowledge that they need in order to produce high performance teams.

Learning about teamwork and developing the skills necessary to create and lead high performance teams, whether they are physical, virtual, functional, cross functional, project or simply one-off task teams, is an absolute essential. A team 'bonding' session in the pub will no doubt be a 'good laugh' but will produce more 'sore heads' than a sustained ability and confidence to guide the team through the recognised team development stages. Conference team-building events such as synchronised drumming, cookery classes, performing the 'haka' or building paper & Lego bridges is simply 'corporate entertainment' and will not deliver the necessary knowledge, confidence, or skill for team managers to create and sustain high performing teams. Experiential team building can work provided the team tasks are appropriate, the facilitation and coaching is first class, and the experiences can be linked back to, and totally related to, experiences in the actual workplace. Vitally they must also produce an action plan that can be worked on when back at work. Having said this, for all this to really work the relevant and basic team 'theories' have to be learned and applied in the first instance.

However, it is not all negative as there are enlightened organisations out there who treat teams and team development seriously and as such ensure that their managers and team leaders have the necessary skills and knowledge about teams and team development. These organisations realise that they must go beyond the traditional leadership courses and they ensure that team development is a core part of their corporate training and development plan. They may even have dedicated team coaches to support this development or in the event of not having this sort of resource internally, they may engage external team coaching expertise as they realise that they need to have their teams performing at the top of their game. This level of high performance is an absolute must if they are to compete at the top level against their competitors in increasingly tough marketplaces.

So, what do organisations have to do to ensure they have continually high performing teams?

1. They must take all their workplace teams seriously. Creating and leading high performing teams is a highly specialised skill that goes beyond just reading from a book or watching a video.

2. Ensure that 'Teamwork Capability' is an essential component of the Company Training Plan.

3. Ensure that, if there is a competency framework for managers and team leaders, then teamworking is a key competency along with the desired behaviours as descriptors.

4. If the organisation has the resources, then look at having dedicated internal capability that can support development of team leadership and teamwork. Failing that, the company must look for external support to assist in developing their teams.

5. Organisations must make sure the basic team development theory is covered utilising all the key developmental models that have been proven to work both in sports and in business.

Even if the organisation is committed to teams and team performance development, the 'stumbling blocks' to implementing team development may actually come from the managers and team leaders themselves. The reasons behind this can be complex and I have outlined the following ten reasons as to why potentially team managers and leaders may not take team development seriously.

1. Many managers will manage and lead their teams based on what they **have experienced as a team member over the years.** The teams they have worked in may have performed and hit their targets and goals and hence the manager may have the mindset that says that if they simply do what the previous manager did, then everything will be all right. Given the fact that true high performing teams are not really that common, then the chances of a new manager having experienced that true top level high performance will be quite low. As such the manager may not be aware that there is a lot more to learn about teams and ensuring the team still grow and can reach their full potential. Organisations should always look to ensure new managers can learn about teams and be supported to be able to lead their teams based on new knowledge and enhanced team development skills. External coaches (or in the bigger companies, internal team coaches) can assist in supporting the development of managers to ensure they are more aware of what knowledge and skill is needed to effectively lead teams to high performance.

2. Following on from Point 1, many managers simply lack **a decent level of knowledge of team dynamics, practical motivation theory and team development models.** As I have mentioned already, many leadership and

management courses touch on team leadership and development, but unfortunately the theory can be limited and there is little emphasis on the practical application of team development and team performance theory. This can easily be rectified as there is an abundance of talent available that can provide development courses and programmes in team development so there can no excuse for not putting in the required support for managers and team leaders.

3. Associated with the lack of knowledge comes **a lack of skill in the art of facilitating and coaching the team.** Many managers still take an 'all encompassing' directive approach as regards all team activity especially meetings activity whereby they create the agenda and then run the whole meeting. If the team is lucky, then perhaps, they will get a say in the agenda and perhaps even set the logistics for the meeting up, but how many managers actually share the leadership of meetings in terms of getting team members to effectively facilitate and run the meetings? Many managers are comfortable coaching their individual team members on a 1:1 basis, but struggle with facilitating and coaching the whole team. Again, this can be easily rectified as there are numerous courses and programmes out there where team managers and team leaders can gain the facilitation and coaching skills required.

4. There are also those managers who **simply do not believe that team and individual performance is enhanced by teamwork.** Many of these managers have not played

competitive team sport (or experienced a true high-performance work team) and as such have not experienced the collective power of individuals really pulling together as a unit. As a result, the belief in teamwork is not as enhanced as it could be. Linked to this as well is also a possible **lack of risk taking** in terms of doing things differently and changing some approaches as to how the team tackle projects, tasks and challenges. A good team coach can work with these managers to work on their self-limiting beliefs as well as also supporting development of their knowledge of teams and team performance.

5. Staying on the belief front, **is the managerial belief that focus on the tasks alone will ensure that the team delivers the results** that are being expected. There is some truth in this in that this provides focus, but if an individual approach is taken then the team could be missing out on more effective and efficient ways of working unless a collective approach is taken. Pulling collectively together will ensure faster development of individual knowledge and skill and should ensure tasks are completed quicker and more creatively.

6. Many managers would like to spend more of their time with the team developing their processes, knowledge and skills but unfortunately **will bow to pressure to have their meetings filled with agenda items that are solely focused on 'business' tasks and 'updates'**. Many of these agenda 'items' will be generated by stakeholders

external to the team, but many managers will accept external requests for time on the team's meeting agenda as opposed to ensuring that there is regular protected time for team development. Seeing agendas change at the last minute to include items that the team do not see as their priority can be very demoralising for teams, so team managers must be able to challenge and influence senior stakeholders to that effect. A good team coach can work with the team leader or team manager to work on their influencing and challenging attitudes and skills.

7. Some teams contain quite challenging characters who are quite prepared to put their views and beliefs forward on a regular basis. Even though this can be done constructively **too many managers would prefer a 'quieter' life and as such will avoid such challenge.** They may even become very directive to ensure no response from the team members. I have seen managers avoid and even cancel team development meetings to avoid such instances and the reasons for the fear can be varied. These reasons can centre around an inability to positively manage the team dynamics and conflict; team challenge can create situations (such as idea generation) that may result in changes to the team operating plan which may cause the manager to have to inform and influence senior management; and there may even be a potential fear of being overshadowed by the more dominant, more experienced, and more capable individual team members. I have had experience of managers simply cancelling team development meetings as

they were afraid that these meetings may expose the manager's failings. I am beginning to sound like a 'stuck record' here but a good team coach or a senior line manager skilled in team coaching can support managers to overcome these fears.

8. There will also be some team managers who **simply lack a decent level of EQ or Emotional Intelligence.** They will possibly have a high IQ, and this may not be matched with the level of EQ required to effectively engage with, and motivate, individuals as well as effectively engaging the entire team on a personal level. These managers relate more to the task involved than they do to the people in the team. They can be masters of process and can make excellent project managers, but leading and managing people effectively can pose a challenge for them and when they are presented with the multiple energies and differing personalities of numerous team members, then this can present real challenges for them. They can resort to micro-management tactics which can and probably will demotivate the team even further and cause further conflict. Team development situations where it is essential for the team to operate at an 'emotional' level can be daunting and intimidating for such managers so there can be a tendency to avoid such situations. Senior managers when recruiting and potentially promoting people into team manager and team leader positions need to ensure that their recruitment processes are of the highest quality so that the right person, with the right capabilities and personality is chosen for the team manager or team leader role.

9. I was made aware of a recently promoted manager who **demanded 'respect' from his team as he was their 'senior' and their 'boss'.** This resulted from the fact that the manager possessed a large ego and with the team being composed of passionate individuals who were keen on putting their ideas forward as well as expressing their frustrations, this proactivity was seen by the manager as a threat to his 'position'. The manager obviously did not like this situation, as in many instances his ideas were being challenged and this was not something he had been used to. As a result, he was not keen on the proposals being put forward as they were not 'his'. He felt that he was not in control of his team and as a result (as he was 'the boss') it was his decision as to how and what the team had to do. The 'I'm the boss' attitude when consistently applied to teams does not work and will result in anarchy and a possible 'overthrow'. I have seen several examples of this happen in my business experience and it usually is caused by a combination of several of the above factors and results in a total task focus and away from any team development opportunities.

10. Unfortunately, and sadly, there are several managers **who simply do not care for their team** (and for the individuals in the team) and as a result little dedicated team development takes place. They have a very selfish individualist approach and are not prepared to support the team or put themselves on the line for the team. When I was a young manager, I remember getting a pretty hard time from a senior manager for the lack of

sales growth that our team was demonstrating. I outlined the key reasons for the lack of growth and outlined the key actions we were taking to increase the growth, but the focus turned to my apparent inability to manage the performance of two of our team who were allegedly struggling. I backed both individuals (who had been Number one and Number two in the company for a different product), but this was seen as being 'weak' by the senior manager. (Nothing could be further than the truth but let us not go there!) After the meeting, a fellow manager said to me that they could not understand why I was 'taking one for the team' as opposed to simply pointing the finger at the two alleged underperformers and saying that I would put them on disciplinary. Their comment of 'you can't let them jeopardise and threaten your position, you have to look after number one' still sticks in my throat, some twenty odd years down the line! My experience of these type of managers thankfully is limited but they are out there, and my own view is that their behaviours need to be challenged by their senior line manager and by their peers. Unfortunately, many senior managers (and peers) will not challenge this type of behaviour as these types of manager are seen to be 'effectively managing performance'. Hmmm.

So, what can be done to ensure team development does happen? Here are four things you can put into action:

1. **Recruit robustly** and ensure team managers are the right people to effectively lead teams to high performance.

2. Make sure you **train and coach** these team managers to have a good knowledge of team dynamics, team models and team performance strategies.

3. **Provide excellent team and 1:1 coaching** (either internally or through external team coaches) to ensure that the skills needed to put the knowledge into practice are developed to the level required.

4. **Provide suitable and motivational incentives** that ensure team development and team performance is rewarded.

With many organisations having 'Teamwork' as one of their core values there can be no excuse to not have team development as one of their development priorities.

So, from both an organisational and an individual team manager and leader perspective, there are many potential 'blocks' to ensuring that team performance development is high on the agenda. What follows in this book is guidance and information as to how you can overcome these blocks by building your knowledge of teams, team dynamics and team performance strategies.

2

Team or Group?
The Performance Curve.

Many groups immediately call themselves a team although in many instances they are not a team and will never actually be a team. It is best to start with the basics and look at exactly what a team is and how this differs from simply being a group. A good way to understand the different types of teams is to look at Katzenbach and Smith's Team Performance Curve. You can find more information with great examples in Katezenbach & Smith's book, 'The Wisdom of Teams'.

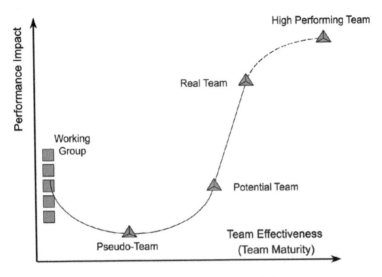

Figure 1 – Katzenbach and Smith's Team Performance Curve from the 'The Wisdom of Teams'.

Let us look at the definitions of each Group / Team.

The Working Group.

- This is a group of people brought together and where there is no significant incremental performance need or opportunity that would require it to become a team, e.g. an advisory group or forum or an action learning set.

- The members interact primarily to share information, best practices, or perspectives and to make decisions in order to help each individual perform within his or her area of responsibility.

- There is no call for either a true team approach or a mutual accountability requirement.

- There is no mutual Team Goal or Objective, and all aspects point solely to individual contributions.

- This is a group for which there could be a significant, incremental performance need or opportunity, but it has not as yet focused on collective performance and may not really be trying to achieve it.
- It has no interest in shaping a common purpose or set of team performance goals, even though it may call itself a team. There will no joint measurement – the focus is on individual performance and measurement. Many sales 'teams' are 'pseudo' teams as the individual sales representatives are only measured on an individual basis and have no measures relating to the overall sales team goals or targets.
- There will be certainly be no team contract in place and activities will be 'manager-led.'
- Pseudo-teams are the weakest of all groups in terms of performance impact and in pseudo-teams, the sum of the whole is purely based on the sum of the individual parts. Given the lack of mutual collaboration and accountabilities the potential of the team is not being fully realised.
- They almost always contribute less to company performance than working groups because there may be an element of individual competition resulting in a lack of sharing success, learning and problem solving.
- For a pseudo-team to have the option of becoming a potential team, the group must define and agree to being measured on specific team goals, so it has something concrete to do as a team that is a valuable contribution to the company.

- In this team, there is a significant, incremental performance shift, and the team is working on improving its overall performance impact.
- The team may still have a need for more clarity about purpose, goals, or work products and more discipline in hammering out a common working approach. If they have not, as yet, put a formal team contract in place, then they should make this a priority.
- Within the potential team there is no established collective accountability and there is still a focus on individual responsibility although more learning and sharing of success is starting to happen.
- More shared leadership and team problem solving will start to help the team 'bond' more effectively.
- The steepest performance gain comes between a potential team and a real team; but any movement up the slope is worth pursuing.

The Real Team

- The real team contains a number of people with complementary skills who are equally committed to a common purpose, goals, and working approach for which they hold themselves mutually accountable. There are joint goals which each team member has an 'attachment' to both psychologically and via measurement.
- Real teams are a basic unit of performance and are forged around an agreed Team Contract.
- There is a continued move towards more increased shared leadership, joint project working and regular performance and contract review sessions.

- Shared learning of both success and failure is the norm with the team having a 'no blame' culture.
- The possible performance impact for the real team is significantly higher than the working group, the pseudo, and potential teams.

The High Performance Team

- This is the team that meets all the conditions of real teams and has members who are also deeply committed to one another's personal growth and success. This is the stage that every team should aspire to.
- There is shared leadership between the team members and regular and structured review of team performance and of their team contract is the norm.
- Peer support and performance review is now accepted and is the norm with the team having a high element of self-direction.
- Team leadership is of the highest quality and its stakeholder management capability is high.
- The high performing team significantly outperforms all other teams, and outperforms all reasonable expectations given its membership and processes.
- It is a powerful unit and an excellent model for all real and potential teams.

There has been work done recently on a further 'level' of team – the e-team or 'Elite' team which is proposed as a level above the high-performance team. In his book "From Mercenaries to Missionaries", former Special Forces soldier, and now internationally acclaimed coach, Martin Murphy, outlines the concept of the Elite team. Martin stipulates that in today's transformation era, we need more than high performance teams and that we need teams to use their collective intelligence to positively influence the strategic direction of the organisation. Details of Martin's book can be found in the bibliography if you want to explore the concept of the e-team.

In addition to the 'Performance Curve,' it is well worth looking at another model of team development and this is the more established model which is quoted in many leadership programmes. This is the Tuckman model of team development and most people will recognise the various stages within the model. These are: Forming, Storming, Norming, Performing and in some instances Adjourning or Dorming.

One of the greatest challenges a team manager has is in moving his or her team though the various team development stages from group through pseudo team, potential team and, real team to a high performing team. If a team manager has no, or little experience of teams and team dynamics then taking over a team and then leading that team can be a stressful experience. Every team manager should know what the various growth stages are of a developing team and they should know how best to move the team through these stages with the minimum of fuss and stress. Unfortunately, many team managers do not get the necessary training or coaching in this area of team development and as such teams go through a lot of angst and turmoil when perhaps this could be minimised quite considerably.

Katzenbach and Smith's Team Performance Curve model along with Tuckman's model will assist the team manager to guide their team through each the development stages and thus minimise the amount of stress that can (and will) occur.

Psychologist, B.W Tuckman developed his team model in the 1970s and Tuckman suggests that there are four key team development stages that teams must go through in order to be productive. The four key stages are:

- **Forming** when the team meets and starts to work together for the first time.
- **Storming**, when the members within the team start to "jockey" for position and when control struggles take place.
- **Norming** when rules are finalised and accepted and when team rules start being adhered to.
- **Performing** when the team starts to produce through effective and efficient working practices.

Some teams will go through the four stages fairly rapidly and move from forming through to performing in a relatively short space of time. A lot depends on the composition of the team, the capabilities of the individuals, the tasks at hand, and of course the leadership from team management. Company culture can also play an important part in how quickly a team moves up the curve and through Tuckman. One thing is certain – no team passes over the storming phase. All teams must be prepared to go through the difficult and stressful times as well as reaping the benefits of the productive phases. The task of the team manager is to identify where along the path of team development his or her team is and then move it on to the next phase with the minimum of fuss and resistance.

If we look at each of the stages in detail.

Forming:

This is a challenging phase when new teams come together. Everyone is a bit wary of each other, particularly if they do not know anyone and particularly if the manager is new. It is even more challenging if the rumours circulating about the manager are not favourable!

The first meeting can be a nervous one and a skilled team manager will recognise this and make attempts to ensure the team is put at ease. As the forming stage is the stage where cliques can develop, the team manager should be aware of this and should be aware of the various alliances that will occur at this stage. Not all alliances will be counter-productive to the team's future success, but it pays for the team manager to watch and observe the behaviours of potential cliques. The challenge for the team manager is basically to give an inert group of people who hardly know each the best start possible as a new team. The team manager should attempt to do the following to give the team the best possible start.

- Outline specifically the goals and tasks the team must perform.
- Be specific about each person's role in the team's goals and tasks.
- Outline how the team has come together and give reasons as to why the various team members have been brought together for inclusion within this team.
- Be open about the way they operate as a manager – what are the manager's strengths and weaknesses? Outline the manager's expectations of both the team and the individuals within the team. In other words, start to contract with the team.
- Encourage each team member to do likewise.
- Ensure that the team has a set of rules and guidelines (team contract) and that the team has an input into how these rules are formed and agreed.
- Discuss reward and recognition. How does the team want to celebrate its achievements?
- How are the team going to make decisions?

- How are the team going to give feedback on each other's performance?

My team development PARTNERS™ is a guide which I would encourage all new teams to follow as it will assist the team to manage the forming stage proficiently. More on this process follows later.

By having an open discussion right at the start of the team's task then people get the chance to air views, concerns and queries. The team manager will enable this to happen with the result that people feel they have been listened to; they have been able to contribute; they know the rules and regulations by which the team will operate, and they now have a greater appreciation of the people they are working with.

Storming:

Storming is a challenging phase and the team manager who has led the team through the forming stage well and is starting to feel quite good about progress may have quite a rude awakening. Storming always seems to come as a surprise, no matter how well the team manager has prepared and led the team up until now. This is where the leadership qualities of the team manager are tested to the full. I have had the privilege of working with some managers who have handled this stage well and I have also witnessed (and suffered) at the hands of team managers who have had no idea of what to do to move the team forward.

Storming usually arises as a result of goals, roles and rules all becoming confused and unclear. No matter how clear the team was in relation to the goals, roles, and rules during the forming stage it is very often the case that the individual team member interpretations of these roles and rules can be somewhat different in reality. This results in confusion when in appropriate behaviours are evident, and conflicts can arise with the potential for factions being created within the team.

It is during this stage that the coaching skills of the team manager should come to the fore. Both individuals and the team should be coached to enable and support them to ensure agreement as regards what specifically the goals, roles and rules are with respect to the team and what that means to each and every individual. Many team managers get frustrated at this stage because they believe that they have already done the work at outlining the goals, roles, and rules at the early stage of the formation of the team. I have seen team managers go from a state of immense pride about the way they have guided their team through the early stages to a state of anger where they look to blame the team and its individual members. Team managers really should look at themselves in terms of well they really did manage to guide the team in the early stages.

The team manager must go over again the agreements made by the team during the forming stage and ensure that the understanding is clear and is uniform across the team. The earlier in the storming stage this is revisited the better and this is where the aware team manager comes into his or her own. The unaware team manager will tend to panic and blame and will be unable to control the behaviours of the team even though they may take a very authoritarian stance and start to order that people behave. All that achieves is reluctant compliance and team members will still have the same misunderstandings about what is going on. This is when a lot of talking goes on "behind the team manager's back". This is very unhealthy for a team and leads to declining performance.

Once the team manager has got his or her team through the storming phase, they need to be aware of a challenge that can come 'out of the blue'. And that is the challenge of a new member joining the team. No sooner has a team manager got their team through the "storm" then it is joined by a new member who then starts to question the ways of working and potentially starts to destabilise the team unintentionally. All new members to the team must be made aware of the team goals, roles, and rules before they join, and they must be made aware of the process that is in place for the giving and receiving of feedback if they have any suggestions as to how they can improve the ways of working for the team. If the team has an already agreed team contract, then the new team member can be taken through this to aid their integration. Again, this is an area where I have seen managers lose the progress that they have made with their team. Instead of taking time out to bring a new member up to speed with all the rules, roles and goals, the manager lets the new member join the team without much of a briefing. The result can be chaos. Beware.

You will find at times that there will be people who tend to hold back the storming process or perhaps prolong it. These people have a decision to make. Go with the majority or get out. Business has no place to let the odd individual hold things up. That message may seem tough coming from a "coaching" team manager, but this is reality, and, in many cases, management is a tough role. This is one of these instances.

Norming.

Do you remember what it is like when a real storm passes? The winds drop, the sky brightens, the birds sing again. Teamwork is like this also. There is a calm, a focus. Goals are clearly understood. Roles are clarified. The rules and regulations are being adhered to and people are working together positively. Relationships become stronger as people are more aware of each other. Strengths and weaknesses are realised and utilised accordingly. Norming is characterised by acceptance. Whereas in the storming stage, people were apt to rebel very quickly, this is now not the case and if someone has a grievance, complaint, or suggestion then the proper processes are used, and people tend to be listened to. The role of the team manager in this stage is to ensure that this calm continues and that any behaviours that arise that may threaten the calm are channelled in the right direction. Also, the team manager has an important role in conveying information particularly in relation to the successes that are starting to occur within the team. The team manager should be spending a lot of time with individual team members coaching them and supporting them to develop their capabilities that relate to the individual's team role and the tasks that they must perform in relation to the team goals.

Performing.

Not every team makes it to the performing stage. Many get stuck at Norming and although everything appears normal, there is a lack of momentum and motivation towards achieving the all-important team goals. It is as though the team is comfortable in this stage and does not want to progress further for fear of returning to a storming stage, a stage that probably was uncomfortable for most people.

It is at the performing stage where team members really concentrate on the team goals. They are determined to work towards them, as they know what rewards are available to them on completion. They are also aware of the strengths and weaknesses of the team, and they appreciate these, and also works towards developing the weaknesses. This is a period of great personal growth among team members. There is a good deal of sharing of experiences, feelings, and ideas together with the development of a fierce loyalty towards team members. There will be arguments, disagreements, and disputes but these will be facilitated positively as the team will now live and die by its team contract. The team manager at this stage will play a non-directive role, concentrating on strategy to plan the next way forward. The team will be in many ways, self-directing, perhaps even self-appraising with the team manager taking a back-seat role. Again, the team manager's role will be to facilitate communication and ensure that the successes are communicated and rewarded.

In summary:

Forming. The team manager will ensure that the team meets and understands the team's purpose, goals, the roles they must take on and the rules by which they must play. The team manager will realise that although there may be a great deal of agreement and compliance about what is discussed many people will have different interpretations of what is agreed. One to ones help but inevitably there will start to be undercurrents of disagreement as to what has exactly been agreed. The construction of a team contract or charter will greatly assist focus and agreed boundaries.

Storming. Once the disagreements and blame start, the team manager should get the team quickly together to thrash out what the concerns and disagreements are. The team manager at this stage is strong, directive but also fair. The team needs direction at this stage and perhaps people need to hear things that perhaps they do not want to hear. Fears and concerns should be voiced constructively and 'out in the open'. The team needs to 'bleed' a little and then begin the healing process by being led effectively to ensure their coming together.

Norming. The team manager lessens the direction and spends time with individuals starting to coach them in relation to their roles within the team and the tasks that they must perform. At the same time, the team manager will be challenging team members to take on extra capabilities to move the team on to the next stage.

Performing. The team manager takes a step back and allows the team to become self-directing. They are 'there' for them and they continue their coaching role with both team and individuals. The team manager should allow individuals to take on leadership roles and encourage rotation of roles. Communication of success is paramount and the rewarding of success imperative.

In Chapter 4 you will come across my PARTNERS™ model which has been designed to ensure that teams have the best possible start to ensure they move up the Team Performance Curve and get through the Tuckman stages of team development with the least amount of resistance. Before that it is important that you gain an appreciation of the key motivational factors that can influence the individual team members.

3

Getting the Basics Right -
ICA, Maslow's & Diamond-
Motivation™

One thing I learned early on when I was being trained as a team coach was that it was essential to have a baseline knowledge of teams and the various models of team dynamics, motivation, and development. As I mentioned in the introduction, I wish that I had been introduced to these in my early days of leading sports teams, and in particular, my first line management appointment in business! I will start first by looking at the very basics of motivation and two key models – the I.C.A model and Diamond Motivation™. I will also make a mention of Maslow's Hierarchy of Needs which is a common model which is trotted out in every leadership and management development course.

Inclusion, Control & Affection

In this chapter I am going to explore an area of teams that team managers are not terribly good at and that is in using the model of "inclusion", "control" and "affection" a model developed by William Shutz, an academic expert on groups.

"Inclusion" is a vital step for a team member to start to function effectively and productively in a team and without this step happening the individual concerned will not function accordingly. New members to a team must be included from the start and they must be made to feel part of the team. Many managers do not take the necessary steps to fully induct people into teams and as such many new team members take time to get functioning. In many cases, if a manager does not pro-actively take steps to ensure inclusion then the other team members may view the new team member with suspicion and distrust. How can anyone function in such an environment?

So, how does the successful team manager manage to include new people to the team right from the start?

Firstly, the team manager should have a "one to one" with the individual concerned. They should outline the aims and objectives of the team, the processes (rules, team contract, boundaries) by which the team operates and then a broad outline of the team members in terms of team roles and experience. Managers should remain silent about their own personal opinions about other team members because if they do not, there is a high chance that the manager's opinions (and perhaps prejudices) will "cloud" the new team member's opinions on future teammates. Not a healthy scenario!

Once this has happened then the team manager will introduce the new member to the team ensuring that beforehand he has spoken to each of the present team to inform them about the new member. The team manager will also ensure that perhaps a "buddy" scheme is set up whereby one team member supports the new person to "find their feet". The manager will also start to facilitate the new person's induction in the team meeting setting by asking them for their input where appropriate. This will put the new person at ease and will make them feel that not only are they being included but also that they are starting to play a role within the team right from the onset. They will start to feel valued.

I have seen too many examples over the years of where "inclusion" has not happened. I have seen managers recruit new team members and send them on initial training courses of up to six weeks duration and never make contact with them – even once! I have seen team managers start team meetings and not even introduce the new member and worst of all I have heard of situations where a new member was given the low down on their new team members in depth with the manager outlining who was good, who was bad, who they should mix with and who they should avoid! How comfortable did you think this new team member felt going to their first team meeting?

Whilst outlining and stressing the role of the team manager in team inclusion, the team manager should also be enabling and supporting the individual to be pro-active themselves. They should be encouraging the new team member to make early contact with the team and to make sure that they made themselves known to teammates at meetings by encouraging them to introduce themselves rather than wait for someone else to do it.

Without "inclusion" many new team members will not only fail to function effectively, but they may also even leave the team! Once inclusion has been achieved then the new team member can go on to the "control" and "affection" stages.

Control

After the members feel "included" within the team, then the dynamics are such that team members can start to exercise a degree of "control". By "control" I do not mean taking over the team. "Control" could mean several things but generally team members can exert control by simply putting their point of view across or, by airing concerns, or by putting forward proposals and suggestions. Too often, although people feel part of the team, in that they "get on well" with the manager and their teammates, people do not feel comfortable in putting across their views, whether they be ideas to move the team forward or whether it is to feedback some constructive criticism. Sometimes this lies with the confidence of the individual team member but in my experience, it generally lies with the team manager taking overall control of the team, doing most of the directing and perhaps not ensuring that individual team members get the opportunity to air their views. The possible result of this 'managerial over-control' is that talented individuals keep their ideas and views to themselves thus preventing the team developing further.

To ensure that each member of the team is able to exert a degree of control, the team manager must be an excellent facilitator. They must be able to ensure that during team meetings team members have their say and are able to put their ideas and suggestions forward. For this to happen the team manager should build (with the team) a "team charter" or "team agreement" whereby the team knows exactly what is expected from them in both team meeting situations and also out-with team meetings. Basically the "team charter" is a form of contract, which outlines how the team is going to operate, both in terms of process and behaviours. When everybody buys into the charter then behaviours improve and ideas, concerns and suggestions tend to come out rather than being only discussed in the "avoid at all cost" "corridor conferences". How many times have you been to a meeting where not much was said by the team during the meeting, but when people broke for a tea-break the level of noise from the team immediately rose! Usually out of earshot of the manager!

So, the successful team manager should facilitate the construction of a team charter and then ensure that this charter is adhered to. The team manager must facilitate their meetings to ensure that all team members get their say on each issue and that every team member gets equal airtime. That means sometimes encouraging certain people to contribute more, and with others, limiting the amount of airtime that they tend to use. Above all the successful team manager must be self-disciplined and not continually "hog the limelight".

Once you have enabled the team to exert "control" you will start to see energy levels rise and the team manager will always have to be prepared, because of this, to ensure that this energy is channelled appropriately. Do not let meetings degenerate into "dumping grounds" where all the issues and all the concerns take over the entire meeting. If there are concerns, then they should be aired, but it is totally counter-productive for the team manager to start to agree with all concerns as this potentially could prevent the team from moving forward. In fact, it may cause the team to go backwards. The team manager in this instance must facilitate and coach the team towards productive and positive outcomes. This is an area where I have seen many team managers come unstuck. They have encouraged the team to be open and when they have been open and honest, (particularly in areas of concern) the team manager has struggled to move the team forward productively in that they can leave the team "hanging". By that I mean, that the team have aired their concerns and although the team manager has listened to them, he or she has moved the conversation on (perhaps to avoid the issues) with a 'pressing' need to get down to "the important business". This must be avoided at all costs as it only serves to increase dissatisfaction. The successful team manager always facilitates and coaches the team to address all the raised issues and work towards a positive outcome.

- Encourage "control" by facilitating the construction and implementation of a team 'contract' or 'charter'.

- Facilitate and coach the team in team meeting situations to encourage participation from all team members. Avoid "hogging the limelight"

- Channel the resultant increase in energy accordingly. Do not leave the team "hanging" on any issue and coach them to productive outcomes, regardless of the issues being raised.

Affection

What do we mean by affection in teams? Affection in some cases will mean love; showing warmth to; a liking towards. And perhaps this is where we start to get it wrong in teams. Affection in the case of teams means simply that we appreciate the contribution of others. It does not mean that we must agree with what others in the team are saying, but what we should appreciate, is the fact that they are contributing both in terms of effort and input of ideas. Too often we are too quick to discount team member' inputs and contributions because we have our own ideas or that, perhaps we have not listened fully to what people have to say.

Once someone is" included" in a team, and then they are able to have a degree of "control", they must be given some "affection". This "affection" may only take the form of listening to ideas and it may only take the form of two words – 'thank-you'. But these two words are probably the most powerful form of motivational feedback there is! Do not underestimate the power of these two simple words – used authentically of course!

If you consider the analogy that the model of Inclusion, Control and Affection is the equivalent of the foundations, structure, and cement of a building then we can start to see why each part of the ICA model is important. Consider, the building. You must have strong foundations. The equivalent of this in a team is the need to ensure everyone is included. Without the team members being included, the result is that they feel isolated and tend to withdraw and their input is lessened thus the team suffers. In a building if you have shaky foundations then the whole structure is put at risk of collapse.

In a building once you have a sound foundation, you must make sure that the supporting structure, in terms of the walls and roof is sound. In a team, the structure must be there in terms of the people and the people not only have to be included, but they also need to have some control. Imagine a building with an insecure wall or roof. How often have you heard the term, "the roof caved in"? The same can be applied to teams. Without giving people some form of control, you may have the foundations of a team, but your whole structure will be very shaky unless you give people the strength by giving them some control.

Finally, in a building once your foundations are laid and you put up the supporting structure, you must secure that structure by the use of cement, glue, nails, and screws. You can do similar with a team by ensuring that affection takes place. Listen to people's contributions. Thank them for them. They may not always be taken up, but at least people will say, "I was given a good hearing". Always thank people for the efforts that they put in. This is the 'cement' that keeps a team together.

Key Points:

- Include everyone from the start. Make them feel

welcome and ensure that each team member includes everyone else.

- Ensure that everyone in the team exhibits a degree of "control" in that they feel comfortable inputting their ideas and contributions.
- Show "affection" by thanking each person for his or her effort and contributions and ideas. Encourage the individuals in the team to do likewise. A good team manager will lead the way but will also encourage participation from each individual team member.

Maslow's Hierarchy of Needs & Diamond Motivation™

A former senior manager from my early days as a sales manager noticed that I had the ability to enthuse and energise our sales team. He asked me how I managed this. I had not really thought about it and it was not until I started to analyse what I was doing, that it dawned on me what I was doing right. There were several things I was doing wrong, too, but we will look at these later.

I asked our team for feedback about what I was doing right when motivating them to work harder and more effectively. This is what they said:

- I took time away from the tasks of the everyday job to sit down with people.
- I listened to them and tried to understand what their hopes and fears were.
- I asked for their opinions on work related matters.
- I asked what their motivators and de-motivators were.
- I managed to link the tasks of the workplace to the benefits to be gained by the individuals.

- I lead by example in attitude and behaviour.
- I was trusted and trustworthy due to my honesty and accountability.

I also asked what they thought I was not doing right in terms of motivating them. They said:

- I was not particularly good at outlining boundaries. People sometimes did not know where they stood and that at times, I was too 'visionary'.
- I trusted people too much.
- I tended to rebel against senior management instead of "managing" them effectively.
- On occasion, I was apt to give advice and tell people what to do instead of guiding them to formulate their own conclusions. When I coached, I was effective but sometimes my impatience led me to be directive when I shouldn't be.
- I was not as effective as I could be when dealing with 'paperwork' and administration.

What does this have to do with motivation? I started to examine this feedback and I could see that if I continued some behaviours and adapted or changed others, I would be able to motivate all individuals in the team and sustain that momentum. The incentive for me was a motivated, responsible, and accountable team who would be productive. This would allow more time for me to concentrate on strategy and facilitating forward movement of the business, as opposed to dealing with conflict resolution and stress management. As a result of improved performance, I could enjoy my time at work more due to the team being productive and enjoying their own work.

To add validity to my coaching approach, I linked this

feedback to models of motivation developed by experts in the field. It would be impossible to review all the models that have evolved on the subject of motivation in this small book, and to me, some of them only confuse rather than enlighten. But I have found two models extremely useful in helping me understand what it takes to motivate an individual or a complete team. They are Maslow's Hierarchy of Needs and Diamond Motivation™

Maslow's Hierarchy of Needs

Abraham Maslow, (1908-70), an American psychologist, and a central figure in the human potential movement, developed a model for motivation which became known as Maslow's Hierarchy of Needs. This is a well-known model, which can be found in books authored by Maslow, books written by his supporters, as well as in textbooks and courses about coaching and motivation.

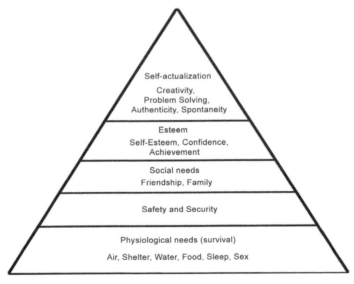

Figure 2 – Maslow's Hierarchy of Needs

This hierarchy is usually depicted as a pyramid with five levels, ranging from the most basic needs – physiological needs – at the bottom, to the most complex and sophisticated needs – self actualisation, at the top with the other three levels filling in the middle. According to his theory, when their most basic needs are met humans will search for self-esteem and self-actualisation. From bottom to top, the levels are these:

- Physiological – air, food, water, sleep, warmth, sex.
- Safety & Security – freedom from fear and violence, shelter, order.
- Social Needs, Belonging – friendship, being in a family, group or team, social acceptance.
- Self-Esteem – self-respect, status, being valued by others.
- Self-Actualisation – need for challenge, variety and growth and need to reach one's full potential.

The goal is to coach (or direct) people at whatever level of Maslow's hierarchy they are in at the present time and help them to "move to the next level" when they are ready. Most people in a work situation will be well above the physiological and safety/security stage with some aspiring towards self-actualisation.

I have seen people fluctuate between the Belonging level and the Self-Actualisation level when they are new employees in the company. Although they might have been operating at the Self-Actualisation level with their previous employers, they may for a time be several steps down in the hierarchy, for example, they may be in the third level: Belonging. Usually this is due to an initial lack of acceptance or welcome from the new team. (Remember the ICA model!)

To motivate these team members, you would not begin by giving them challenging tasks, because you would potentially de-motivate them. What they need is a chance to become accepted in their new environment. They need to be introduced to work colleagues, team members, and superiors, and to learn their new jobs and make friends at work. Once they are established with their peers and their work expectations, they can move to the next level: Self Esteem. When this level is achieved and the new employee is assimilated in their new place with the help of a nurturing, supportive, coach they may eventually be ready to move towards Self-Actualisation. This is the level all organisations should be aiming to get their employees into and then maintain them there.

I have seen previous employers lose some high class, top-quality people who were regularly in the Self-Actualisation level. These people appeared to have slipped down the hierarchy towards the Self-Esteem level and in some cases to the Belonging level. This happens when management is not using their employees' full potential by not including them in decision-making and other situations (such as shared leadership) that would give them more responsibility. The management of the company, for example, may have been experiencing problems from a transition after a merger. The manager may have assumed that because these people were "top class" they would "continue to perform with little guidance." If this is the case, then the management team has missed a vital step in motivating employees by making assumptions about people's level of motivation. Again, communication skills, such as, feedback, listening, and coping with stress might have helped in this case.

The second model I use is:

Diamond Motivation™

Several years ago, I had the pleasure of sharing the conference stage with Great Britain Olympic athlete, Brian Whittle, and

Brian introduced me to a simple model of motivation entitled the 'Motivational Triangle' where the model stipulated that there were three distinct motivators that all humans needed addressed before they could be fully motivated.

- Understanding and Being Understood.
- Freedom to Choose.
- Feeling Valued.

I would like to further explain this powerful model in an enhanced form I have developed called 'Diamond Motivation ™' and which adds an important and crucial fourth dimension to Brian's model. This model can be used for both individual and team development and can also be used as a framework for organisations when attempting to create a 'culture of empowerment'.

Let us look at how this simple model of motivation applies to enabling team managers to support their team members, and for all team members to use it to be self-motivated.

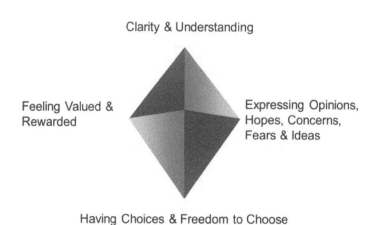

Clarity & Understanding

Feeling Valued & Rewarded

Expressing Opinions, Hopes, Concerns, Fears & Ideas

Having Choices & Freedom to Choose

Figure 3 – Diamond-Motivation™

It is vital for any team member to have clarity in what their role is, and what their performance measures and targets are. Without this clarity the team member will be potentially confused and de-motivated. Team Managers should always ensure that team members have 100% clarity in the following areas, 100% of the time!

- An excellent understanding of company and team purpose and goals and how their objectives link to the overall purpose and goals of the team.
- Clear and concise description of their role and responsibilities within the team.
- Clear on their individual SMART objectives.
- Clarity in relation to how best they are going to achieve the objectives and what support is available from the team manager.
- A full knowledge and understanding of company and team procedures and policies.
- A full understanding and commitment to the team contract.
- An understanding of how best the Team manager: Team member relationship is going to work for both parties.
- A full understanding of all reward and recognition processes.

Expressing Opinions, Hopes, Fears, ideas, and Concerns

The second aspect to 'Diamond Motivation™' is that humans need to express themselves. If they are dictated to, then, not only do they feel under-valued, but they also feel frustrated in that they are not offered the opportunity to outline their hopes, ideas, fears, and concerns.

Team Managers should always ensure open two-way communication and be excellent listeners. A healthy balance of being directive and of 'playing the coach' should be aimed for so that the correct developmental approach is taken at the right time and situation. Taking a coaching approach will ensure that employees are given opportunity to convey their feelings, hopes, concerns and ideas and team managers should always attempt to ensure that situations are created where employee views are aired and heard. Simply being the 'directive' team manager is fraught with danger in that this approach can severely restrict and impact negatively, this aspect of 'Diamond Motivation™. Team Managers should always look to have their coaching and situational leadership skills enhanced. This focus of this book is on team performance but more in-depth information on how to develop individual coaching skills can be found in my first book, "The Successful Coaching Manager". Details can be found, along with other excellent books on coaching in the Bibliography.

Having a Choice in Decisions

People need to be able to make choices. Some people need a lot of scope in this area, others only a little. But choices must be offered and created and the best way to do this is for the team manager to coach effectively whereby the team member comes up with their own solutions and ways to implement the solutions. Simply telling team members what to do and how to do it can have little effect, apart from perhaps, a negative effect! There are instances, though, when being directive is the right developmental approach. Check out the 'Skill / Will Matrix' (Capability – Motivation Grid) in 'The Successful Coaching Manager'.

Team Managers should also look to create focus and problem-solving groups to enable team members to look closely at workplace challenges and come up with their own recommendations. This can go some way to satisfying the human need to have choice.

Feeling Valued and Recognised

There are some extremely simple ways to make someone feel valued. It is as simple as saying 'thank you' and 'well done'. It is also extremely powerful to simply listen and understand someone and this process alone is a sure way of making someone feel valued. And so, with team members – listen to them, understand their needs, support them to make decisions and thank them for their effort and expertise in the workplace. Simple.

Why is it that so many team managers severely limit praise but immediately focus in on mistakes? This must change if we are to be able to make full use of 'Diamond Motivation™'

Motivation is key in everything we do. Maslow's Hierarchy of Needs and the other motivational theories are useful, but "Diamond Motivation™" simplifies the mystique and takes motivation to a personal level which is easy to understand and apply.

Getting the Basics Right – PARTNERS™

In Chapters 1 and 2, I introduced the Team Performance Curve and Tuckman Team Development Models which highlighted the various 'stages' that various 'teams' go through before achieving true high performance. Whilst I was aware that guidance was given in a lot of team literature which gave team managers and team leaders pointers to what exactly to do to move the team through the various stages I felt that the guidance lacked a definite structure, and this is the reason I have created the PARTNERS™ Accelerator process. If you follow this process as a 'start-up' guide and also use it as an assessment tool for your reviews, then you will be in a great position to move the team up the performance curve and through the Tuckman stages seamlessly.

Below is a summary of the PARTNERS™ process and the main points at each stage in the process.

	Overview of Stage	Main Aims of each Stage
P	P = PURPOSE	Many teams do not know exactly what the team purpose is as they can get bogged down in trying to work out a team vision and mission. Visions and missions do not always apply to every team but every team regardless of seniority has a purpose. The team members may be aware of what they must do individually but struggle when asked what the overall purpose of the whole team is. It is vital that this is understood by all team members and not just by the manager or team leader
A	A – AIMS, GOALS AND TARGETS.	What are the team's specific aims, goals, and targets? Most teams are brought together to deliver outputs, and these tend to be short term (up to a year) in the main although larger project teams can have goals and outputs which are of a greater duration. The key here is to ensure 100% clarity as to what the specific goals for the team are and what each individual's aims, and goals are and how they are being measured.
R	R – RELATIONSHIPS, ROLES & RESPONSIBILITIES	Does everyone understand their specific roles and responsibilities? Do they know their specific objectives and measures aligned to their role and responsibilities? What are the various personality styles and how well do they fit together in the team? Have each person's strengths been identified and are they being used to their full effect within their roles?
T	T – TRAINING & RESOURCES	Are there any major training needs and does the team have all the resources they need to achieve their goals and targets? There may be a training need for the whole team but also individual needs that need addressed in order that everyone can achieved their agreed goals and objectives.

	Overview of Stage	Main Aims of each Stage
N	N – NEEDS	It is vital that the team has an agreement in place that highlights how best they are going to work together. This achieved by establishing what each team member needs personally to work productively within the team. Once these are established then a review of what has worked well and not so well within the team can be established. It is also important that individual values are outlined so that awareness of individuals' preferences is increased across the team.
E	E – EXPECTATIONS & EMPOWERMENT	What are the expectations of the manager or team leader of the other team members? What are the Team's expectations of the manager or team leader? What are the levels of empowerment? What can be done without referral to the manager? What needs consultation and what needs full approval? Once there is agreement and expectations managed then these can be added to the team 'contract'. It is also important to discuss how decisions are going to be made within the team.
R	R – REWARD & RECOGNITION & REVIEW	What reward and recognition processes are needed in order that the team pulls cohesively and productively together? What review processes will be agreed and at what frequency? How will the team review the overall progress towards the team goals?
S	S – SUPPORT & STAKEHOLDERS	What support processes must be put in place to support the team towards its goals and targets? Who are the team's key stakeholders and how are they going to be managed & influenced?

Let us look at each of the stages in detail and focus on the first two elements of the PARTNERS™ process – the P and the A. But before that, let us discuss V and M – Vision and Mission. I have been a member of many business (and sports) teams over my working life and I have also been involved in supporting teams to develop their processes as an external coach. On the occasions I have been involved in teambuilding exercises, the starting point for the team was to create a 'Vision and Mission' statement. Personally, I now believe that in many team cases this is a waste of time, energy and probably money. Whilst I believe that having a vision and a mission is important, I believe this should be reserved for the very top team in corporations to work on and does not apply to everyday work teams such as sales teams or manufacturing teams where the focus is on short to medium term 'deliverables. For example, I have worked as an employee for 6 companies since 1982, each one of whom had a vision and a mission statement. I cannot remember any of these vision statements now and to be honest I could not remember them word for word when I worked for them! There was one company whose vision statement appealed to me (or at least a small section of it did) and this was because it really was aligned with my values but as for the other company visions – I simply cannot remember them. I do remember though, taking a lot of time (and expense) in engaging external facilitators to build a vision and mission statement for some of the sales teams that I was leading, and whilst we got there in the end (with a nice laminate and logo) it was a painful process that in fact was ultimately a waste of time as two weeks down the line no one could remember exactly what the vision was, and what the mission statement said! Individual team members in the vast majority of business teams may relate (in part) to big fancy vision and mission statements but ultimately what drives an individual member of a team is a real understanding of what the team's actual purpose is and what the team's overall aims, goals and objectives are. This is what any team leader or team manager should focus on at the start of any teambuilding. Do not waste time on fancy and expensive vision and mission statements – that is unless you are the top leadership team or board of directors where it is expected that you build that vision and mission for your organisation.

So, what exactly is a 'team purpose'? The purpose of any team is its reason for being. Now team members can sometimes get confused as to what the fundamental purpose of their team is. For example, I was reminded of a situation a former colleague was involved in a couple of years back, when they were asked to join a project team looking at launching key account management as a new way of working for the organisation. The remit was for the project team to launch a 'playbook' around key account management so that the company employees would understand what key account management is, and how this way of working would benefit the organisation as a whole. This was to be launched at the company's annual conference, where all company employees would be present. The project team got to work and immediately flew into task to produce the 'playbook' (don't you just love this terminology?) and then the team worked on how this would be presented at the conference. A glossy 'playbook' was duly produced, and an upfront slide presentation of the 'playbook' was delivered from the stage to the audience. Job done! Unfortunately, the feedback rating was 3 out of 10 (the lowest rating of the conference) with the audience feeling preached at, and patronised, with the result that they did not engage with the process. It meant that the implementation of new working practices (which would benefit the whole of the organisation) were now being seen as negative as opposed to the original intention. On reviewing the situation with my former colleague, it became very apparent that the project team had focused very much on the tasks at hand and had not taken the time to work on the actual purpose of the team's remit. On reflection the actual purpose of the project team was not simply to produce a key account management 'playbook' and present it at conference, the purpose was to ensure that the company employees saw key account management as a new exciting working practice that was of real benefit to all the company's employees regardless of what function they worked in. The 'playbook' and the conference presentation were only to be important 'vehicles' for realising the team's purpose. If the project group had focused on engaging the organisation as to their purpose and the purpose of key account management, then they would have achieved a much better launch of the initiative.

Agreeing and fully understanding what the overall purpose of the team is, will ensure that the specific aims, goals, and objectives are the right ones to ensure the team's clear and compelling purpose is realised. A clear and compelling purpose will provide a strong source of meaning and significance for the team members in relation to the aims, goals and objectives that have been set for the team.

Now that the team has discussed and agreed its overall purpose, the team can get down to looking at the aims, goals and objectives that need to be achieved to fulfil their purpose. The purpose gives meaning to the aims and goals, but the aims, goals and objectives start to give the team real focus on what it needs to deliver. Again, it is vital that these aims, and goals are fully understood right from the onset. I used to be amazed when some salespeople in the sales teams I was coaching could not remember exactly what their overall aims and goals were! One of the reasons for this was that the work had not been done at the start of the team's formation to really ensure that everyone fully understood the team's purpose and the specific aims and goals needed to achieve that purpose.

Again, time should be taken to ensure that the team's aims, and goals are S.M.A.R.T. Most people will know that this means: S – Specific, M – Measurable, A – Achievable, R – Realistic / Relevant, and T – Time bound. The term C-SMART is banded about a lot where the C stands for Challenging but I have seen team managers 'abuse' this to the extent that they overstretch their team to the point of 'collapse' and any decent manager with coaching capability will be able to build in an appropriate 'stretch' within the actual S.M.A.R.T process.

If we look at our key account management project team outlined earlier the key aims and goals for the team should have been as follows:

1. To ensure that the organisation, fully understands and 'buys' into what key account management is and how it will benefit both employees and the overall organisation – August xxxx Conference.

2. To design a key account management 'playbook' outlining what key account management is and how it can be implemented effectively with the organisation. By end June xxxx

3. To prepare an impactful and engaging conference presentation and workshop outlining what key account management is and how it will benefit the organisation and its employees by end July xxxx

4. To deliver an impactful and engaging presentation at the August conference that will enthuse and engage the audience into believing that key account management is the way forward for the organisation.

5. To ensure employee satisfaction with the conference presentation with a score of 8/10. Feedback forms to be sent out immediately post conference and

results analysed and communications two weeks after the August conference.

So, we now have a project team who have a clear purpose and have specific aims and goals that are aligned to the purpose. The next step is to ensure that the various actions needed to achieve the purpose and aims are put in place via the team members.

Questions & Actions:

1. Revisit the actual Purpose of your team. Is this purpose fully understood by all your team members? Do you as team leader understand exactly what the purpose is?
2. What the specific aims and goals for your team? Are these S.M.A.R.T and are these fully understood by all team members?
3. Are the aims and goals fully aligned to the team's overall purpose?

This may seem all very straightforward, but you would be amazed just how many teams simply fly into task without fully understanding what the team's purpose and specific aims and goals are. This does not assist in enabling the team to gel together and ensuring they have real focus on delivering against their aims and goals. This can also cause extra challenges for the team when the team starts to enter the 'storming' phase of team development.

PARTNERS™ - Roles and Responsibilities & Training

Whilst all aspects of the PARTNERS™ process are important if the team is going to hit high performance, the understanding of the roles and responsibilities of each team member is crucial if you are to navigate the team through the 'storming' phase of Tuckman's model.

This is the stage where it is imperative that everyone in the team knows what their role is and what specific responsibilities, they have in order that every member of the team pulls together to hit the team and individual goals. This may seem straightforward, but it is always best to fully check that every team member knows exactly what they must achieve. You will be amazed how many assumptions are made based on misunderstandings of what needs to be done and this can cause turmoil later down the line. The other key challenge I have come across frequently is where a team is composed of similar roles and as such the role has a list of 'standard' objectives and measures otherwise known historically as the 'job description'. Sometimes this can be slightly different from the actual list of responsibilities agreed so this needs to be discussed and agreed right at the start with any major differences highlighted to senior management and / or Human Resources. Good team managers can handle this, poor team managers stick to the company job description and this is not conducive to effective team performance.

I have found the best way to achieve clarity right across the team in terms of roles and responsibilities is to discuss this openly as a team with every member having an awareness of what each team member is having to achieve. The team leader or manager should lead the way and openly discuss what their own responsibilities and objectives are. This starts to build real trust within the team, and this is essential if the team is to pull through the storming phase together and progress to high performance. If you are a manager who is not prepared to share your own specific responsibilities and objectives with your team openly then I would suggest team management and team leadership is not for you. Whilst teams need strong direction through this early 'storming' phase it should be done in a collaborative and open fashion with the team manager showing strong leadership which includes being open about their own objectives. We will discuss this more when we look at expectations.

It is always good at this point to do a 'strengths' exercise with the team to identify where each team members' 'strengths' and 'weaknesses' lie. This can be vital so that you can align team members' key strengths with specific team projects and tasks. Occasionally it is useful to align projects and tasks that have a particular skillset to team members who are looking to develop in possible 'weak' areas, but care should be taken to ensure that some form of support is in place to allow them to develop their 'weak' areas, preferably through some form of mentorship and or joint project working with someone who has the requisite strengths required. Do not simply leave individual members to get on with projects which need specific skills that are not focused on the team member's particular strengths. This is tantamount to potential disaster on several fronts. There is a chapter dedicated to 'strengths' in this book written by Strengths expert, Trudy Bateman.

At this stage it is also important that the team start to explore exactly how each member is going to work on their responsibilities and objectives. This should be done initially as a team to establish whether there are any overall Training needs that the whole team needs to work on and as such a team training or development plan should be put in place. In terms of individual training needs (outside the overall team training plan) then these can be identified in the 1:1 coaching sessions between the team manager and the individual team member. The important thing to ensure here is that both the team training plan and the individual training plans stay 'alive' and do not simply gather 'dust' in a file on a computer hard drive or in an HR online framework! Whilst regular team reviews will focus on the how the team is progressing towards hitting its aims and goals, it is vital to ensure that time is put aside to ensure a regular training plan update.

Key points to consider:

- Ensure absolute clarity right across the team in terms of every team member individually knowing their roles and responsibilities and those of their fellow teammates.
- As the team manager, lead the way and share your specific responsibilities and objectives so that the team know what you are working on what you are aiming to achieve.
- Consider doing some 'strengths' profiling of the team to make sure that each team member's strengths are aligned to the projects that are expected to undertake.
- If a team member is going to be working on a project and the skills needed are outside their 'strengths' areas, then consider some form of support either in partnership working or having them assigned a mentor.
- Develop a team training plan covering those key development areas that run across all the team members and ensure each team member has their own individual training plan with actions.
- Ensure the training plans are reviewed regularly as a team and in 1:1 coaching sessions.

Getting absolute clarity on the purpose, the aims and goals of the team and the individual roles and responsibilities of all team members is critical in preparing the team to enter the 'storming' phase of team growth.

*"The strongest team leaders
know exactly what their team
members actively need."*
Anon.

This next stage of the PARTNERS™ process is the 'personal' stage and every team member should be given the opportunity to discuss their key values and what their specific needs are in terms of working within a team. Everyone will have experiences of working in successful teams and will no doubt have opposite and differing experiences where they have worked in unsuccessful teams, and where the culture is not conducive to enabling high performance. It is vital to start to get the team discussing openly their experiences and you should run a session where each person gets the chance to explain what it was like working in a great team and similarly what it was like in the unsuccessful team. What behaviours were on display in each? What attitudes did the team members in each team have? What was the atmosphere like in each team? How did each individual feel about working in the teams? Get the team members to also highlight what their key values are, and what they would want their present team to be like in terms of consistent behaviours & attitudes. Once this is discussed and the information collected in the team session you can then start to build a team 'contract' or 'charter'. This is simply an agreement put together by the team which details the purpose, aims and goals of the team along with the behaviours and attitudes that the team needs to display to hit the aims and goals. I've seen some pretty complicated contracts so my advice is to keep it simple so that it 'lives' and can be reviewed easily! And please, please, please make this a full team exercise! I have experienced team managers delegate this task to the team while they avoided the exercise totally. This is unacceptable and if any team manager does this then I would implore the team to challenge the team manager, constructively, of course!

After having the 'needs' discussion, the next step is to be upfront about what the expectations are between team manager or team leader and the rest of the team. This is a crucial exercise because it is vital that there is absolute clarity around what the manager or leader expects from the team and similarly what the team expects from the manager. To give you an example of what 'expectations' look like, as a line manager I always expected an individual's expenses to be completed diligently and by the deadlines agreed. I also expected that if someone in the team was struggling with deadlines (or anything for that matter) to be upfront and to contact me to see how I could support getting the deadline hit or discuss an extension of the deadline. As regards the members in the team, their expectations were that I would be open to the discussions and look to fully understand reasons as to why deadlines might not be hit.

Once the expectations are 'out in the open' then discussions can be had around what exactly each expectation looks like and a solid agreement can be put in place between the manager or team leader and the team members. In other words, the expectations can be managed and agreed. There should now, be no surprises later down the line! This is an excellent exercise to continue to build trust within the team and I have seen and experienced some excellent sessions where the result has been the removal of a lot of the 'apprehension' around how, for example, a new manager operates. I've also experienced the opposite where the manager has shied away from such discussions, only to use this 'lack of awareness' to their own advantage, as one manager highlighted to me, "to keep them on their toes". Good grief. It was no surprise that this team manager had a high turnover rate of staff and was eventually removed from their managerial post.

The key to any successful team contract and agreed expectations (the expectations could be included in the overall contract) is to make sure all team members keep to the desired behaviours and attitudes that have been agreed. The team should also openly discuss what happens if a particular team member 'breaks' the contract or doesn't keep to the expectations and a feedback process should also be agreed.

Some Suggestions and Action Points:

- In your early meetings with the team once you have agreed purpose, aims, goals, roles, and responsibilities consider an open session looking at each person's individual values and needs of working in a high-performance team.
- Create a team contract or agreement that everyone inputs to and can be reviewed easily.
- Agree a review process and timetable to keep the contract alive.
- Outline the team manager or leader's expectations of the team and allow the team to do similar. Make sure there is agreement all round and add this to the contract if the team feels it fits in there.
- Discuss and agree a feedback process if any team member 'breaks' the contract.
- Above all make sure that everyone sticks to the contract!

PARTNERS™ – Review, Reward and manage Stakeholders.

So far, we have covered the vital importance of team having an agreed Purpose, having joint Aims and goals, ensuring clarity over Roles and Responsibilities, a robust Training plan, and have ensured that all team members' Needs, and Expectations have been openly discussed and built into a Team Contract or Charter. We can now look at how the team must Review, Reward and at the same time manage their Stakeholders so that every element is now in place on the road to high performance.

PARTNERS™ - Make Sure Review Happens!

I have lost count of the number of times team managers have put the effort into ensuring the team get off to the best possible start. The team have taken time out to discuss how the team is going to work together; they have put a development or training plan in place as well as in some cases, a team contract, and then they simply forget to review the plan and contract as the work year progresses. The reasons cited by team managers inevitably centre on being 'too busy' due to 'priorities', 'urgent initiatives' or simply not enough time due to "senior management' demands". Let me make the point clear. If you are going to put in place a process like PARTNERS™ to get your team off to the best possible start, you need to review the team's progress at reasonably regular intervals. You would not forget to review the business plan so why forget to review the team plans that will, in many ways underpin the delivery of the business plan?

In terms of timescales, I would suggest that at the very minimum, team managers should consider a mid-year review and a year-end review although ideally a quarterly review should be considered. The best review process I have encountered is where the team (and this was a new start team) put the team development plan and contract in place at the start of the year, January – had informal reviews in March and September with more formal reviews in June/July and then in December. The December meeting doubled as a review of the previous year as well as adjusting the development plan for the following year. This meant that come the start of the new year they were ready to go.

Please do not forget the team development plan and contract – it truly does underpin how the team's work or business plan is delivered!

PARTNERS™ - What about Reward & Recognition?

This is an area where organisations can really struggle. A great many organisations talk about teams and then only put reward and recognition initiatives in place that reward and recognise individuals. This can create internal competition as individuals vie for 'top spots' and as a result, individuals are reluctant to share information and learning from successes. This can be prevalent in those organisations who run individual performance 'league tables' and this can lead to destructive team behaviours. A manager I encountered a while back actually stopped joint project working because it was easier to manage and reward people individually as opposed to working out what each person had done within the project. This manager missed out on a real trick as the previous joint working meant team members were working to their strengths as opposed to being left to run projects on their own.

Whilst putting in place reward schemes are fraught with challenges, they are essential in terms of teamwork and very often it is the simple schemes that make the biggest impact. 'Team of the Year' schemes where the reward is for some form of 'trophy' and perhaps a team meal out or team event can be immensely powerful. Just the pure recognition with not even a hint of monetary reward can be enough to pull a team together and enable them to focus on what needs to be done to win. Keep it simple and forget complex mathematical scoring systems that team members do not understand. The more complex a scheme is, the more likely the team will lose interest in the scheme altogether. We live in a complex enough world without having to have a degree in astrophysics which will allow us to decipher the latest team incentive! The simpler the better but it must have real meaning for the team and a lot will depend on just how the company champions the scheme and how inspirational the team manager is in supporting and enabling the team to buy in to the scheme. Reward and Recognition is discussed in more detail in a later chapter.

PARTNERS™ - Forget Stakeholders at Your Peril!

This is an area of influence that many teams do not even consider. And yet, the area of stakeholder management is crucial to the how the team is perceived and supported particularly in terms of reward schemes! Many teams will take serious time to map out their external 'customers' in the form of a 'stakeholder map' and work out how they are going to influence these customers and how each customer stakeholder can support their business. Teams should be doing this for their 'internal stakeholders' also. Senior stakeholders can be a great support to the team and if teams are going to be hugely successful, they should be looking to manage their key internal stakeholders across the associated functions in the business. Perception is key and as a 'perception is a person's reality' then that reality needs managed and influenced so that the team is seen in a positive light by all key stakeholders. As part of the PARTNERS™ process an internal stakeholder map is always discussed and discussions held as to how the team can rally support from stakeholders across the business.

- Make sure the team reviews progress of the team development plan and team contract at regular intervals.
- Keep Reward and Recognition schemes simple.
- Create a Key Stakeholder Map and make sure this reviewed as part of the review process.

The PARTNERS™ **Accelerator** process when applied rigorously and reviewed routinely will provide the essential basic foundations that will move the initial group of people up the performance curve whilst going through the various stages of team development. Importantly it will enable the team to navigate the most challenging stage, that of the 'storming' phase. Many teams will struggle through this stage and I have seen many teams unable to break out of this stage and can be permanently stuck there. This is an extremely uncomfortable state to be stuck in!

5

The Team Contract & Team Development Plan

Many teams go through their entire existence without a formal team contract or team development plan. These teams are missing a huge 'trick' because formalising their 'modus operandi' and having a structured development plan can really mean the difference between being a real team and a high performing team. Having the formal contract and development plan ensures the team is continually developing its skills and knowledge as well as preventing any untoward behaviours getting out of hand. Whilst many teams who have a verbal team contract and individual development plans can get to a decent level of performance with excellent leadership, they may well not be fulfilling their true potential and the more formal approach of having a structured, written, and reviewed team contract and development plan could make that extra 1% of a difference towards high performance.

So, what exactly is a team contract or charter? This is simply a formal document that outlines what the team is aiming to achieve and what behaviours are going to be demonstrated by all team members, consistently, competently, and confidently. You can make the team contract as simple or as complicated as you want to, but the key thing is to ensure that there is full team agreement as to its contents and to its review. In many ways this is the team's own 'operational manual'. You can use the PARTNERS™ process to assist in your structuring of the contract and an example of a straightforward team contract is the example below from the Leadership Team of The University of Glasgow's Men's Rugby Club. My thanks go to the leadership team for allowing me to publish an abridged version of their contract.

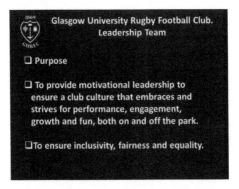

Figure 4 – GURFC Contract – Purpose

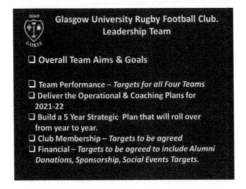

Figure 5 – GURFC Contract – Aims & Goals

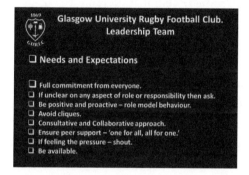

Figure 6 – GURFC Contract – Training Needs

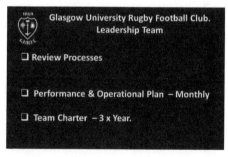

Figure 7 – GURFC Contract – Needs and Expectations

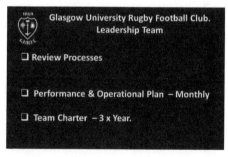

Figure 8 – GURFC Contract – Review Process

As you can see the team have decided to focus on their purpose, goals and 'needs' and 'expectations' along with an agreed review process. Their larger version also outlines each the roles of responsibilities within the team and they thought this was important as their team is transient with new people coming into the positions every year. Having this documented in the contract meant that everyone in the club has a full understanding of what is entailed in each role ensuring that new team members can understand their roles and responsibilities quickly.

This contract is also shared with the whole club membership to drive and ensure full accountability of the leadership team members in the eyes of the people they are 'leading'. How many senior leadership teams in organisations have (a) a team contract and how many (b) actually share it with the whole organisation?

There are many other examples of team contracts to be found on the internet so simply do a 'Google' and you will get access to them. The important thing is that you document your discussions and formalise them. Some teams have all their team members sign their team contracts to get that 'physical' as well as 'mental' commitment to them.

The Team Development Plan

This is the plan that will ensure your team's skills and knowledge are at the level required to deliver the team's purpose and its aims and goals, and as such ensure that the team is performing as a high-performance team. The secret to this plan is twofold: firstly, keep it focused on priority development areas that apply to the whole team; and secondly ensure that it is reviewed on a regular basis.

Table 1 gives an example of a simple template that can be used and one which will not be new to any experienced team manager. The crucial thing is to ensure it is populated and then executed with regular review along the way!

Team Development Goal	Actions	Team Member Leads	By When?	Complete?
To Develop Omni-Channel Sales Skills of Team	Develop Individual development plan with sales coach	Team Manager	Ongoing	
	Organise team development day on remote selling and follow up coaching	Account Manager 1 with Company Training Manager	1st March	
	Remote Team sessions to back up company e-learning	Account Manager 2 with Company Training Manager	Every two weeks from 1st March until 1st May	
	Agree team list of questions that can be posed to key customers virtually and have team session of practice asking the questions.	Account Manager 3 with Regional Manager	1st February	

Improve Account Planning Capability across all team members	Team session to support each team member's capability in creating account plans	Account Manager 4 with Company Business Analyst	12th February	
Create Formal Team Contract	Team session with external coach input	Regional Manager with External Coach	19th February	
Create a detailed Stakeholder Management plan	Run a session on stakeholder mapping	Regional Manager	24th March	
Hold Peer Assessment Review Meetings	Presentation from external coach experienced in peer review. Run session on giving and receiving feedback	Regional Manager with Company Training Manager & External Coach	2nd April and 2 x sessions within the year. (Dates to be agreed)	

6

Awareness of
Team Personalities

I always suggest to teams that it is important that all team members have a full appreciation of each team member's preferred behavioural style and of their key strengths.

This chapter will give you greater understanding of behavioural or personality styles and suggest ways that you can flex your own style to build rapport with your team members. Flexing one's style can, under certain conditions, be difficult and tiresome, for example, in the case of dealing with people under stress. It is vital though, that a team manager leads the way and always maintains rapport with all team members. I have seen too many team managers refuse to change their style because their ego tells them that the team members should be flexing towards their style since they are "the boss". Get a Life! The result is usually a "personality clash" and perhaps you can guess who stands to lose the most in that situation. However, if all team members have the same knowledge of behavioural styles, they can learn to flex and accommodate too, especially with their own team, colleagues, and customers. This will make it easier for everyone involved.

What are these behavioural styles, how do you identify them, and how do you adapt your style to others'? There are numerous models of behavioural styles and they are all based on work done in the 1920's by the psychologist, Carl Jung. It would be beneficial for you to read more about his work as well as familiarise yourself with the various models, such as: Myers-Briggs Type Inventory (MBTI) and The Disc Personality Type – (Dominant, Influencing, Steady, Cautious) – DISC and the various 'offshoots' of these.

The Four Behavioural Styles

There has been a lot of research on behavioural style, producing many models, but they are all remarkably similar in a variety of ways. The model I will introduce you to was developed by Wilson Learning in the United States (www.wilsonlearning. com). It is the one I have used most in my career, and I find it works well particularly in team situations. I also like the work of Dr. Michael Lillibridge entitled The People Map because it uses up-to-date and corporate language. A more visual model was created by the Insights Organisation (www.insights. com) using four different colours to represent each of the four predominant styles and another recent development is around work done by Olav Kyrre Fjeld (www.teamhuset. com) which combines the four personality type model with aspects of the Myers-Briggs Type Inventory. All of these should be explored to see which model sits most comfortably with your organisation.

Both the Wilson Learning and Lillibridge models suggest that there are four distinct behavioural types. For each of us, our behavioural style can be viewed as our personal comfort zone, or the style we adopt most naturally when not under stress.

Labels are used to identify these four behavioural styles; however, they are only labels. It is most important to be aware of the characteristics of each, and not the definition of the word itself. It is also important to note there will be some crossover, in almost everyone; therefore, there are no absolutes. Some characteristics will be far more prominent in some people's normal behaviour than in others. Everyone is a mixture of the styles with each individual having a different 'mix'.

Driver, Controlling, or Leader Style

People who fit into this category are business-like and formal in appearance. Their main priority is the task at hand, and the results achieved. Their pace is fast and decisive. They prefer an atmosphere in which they can control people and processes and achieve acceptance through their productivity and competitiveness.

Drivers like to be in charge, seek productivity, and dislike loss of control. They want you to get to the point because they are irritated by inefficiency and indecision. They measure their personal worth by the results they achieve, and their track record. Under pressure these people will assert themselves strongly and dictate the way things are going to be – they are autocratic.

To influence and work with these people, support their goals and objectives, and demonstrate what your ideas will do, when you will do it, and the cost. They want results.

Analytical, Processing, or Task Style

People using this style appear somewhat formal and

conservative. Their main priority is the job at hand, and the process needed to achieve it. Their pace is measured and systematic. They prefer an atmosphere that encourages careful preparation and achieves acceptance through being correct, logical, and thorough.

Analyticals want recognition for being correct, seek accuracy, and dislike embarrassment. They want you to be precise in your dealings with them because they are irritated by unpredictability and surprises. They measure their personal worth by their degree of precision, accuracy, and activity.

Under pressure, these people will withdraw into their own world, and avoid contact with causes of stress.

To influence and work with this personality, you need to support their thinking, and show how your ideas will support their personal credibility.

People, Amiable, or Supporting Style

People Style individuals appear to be casual but conforming. Their pace is slow and easy. They prefer to maintain relationships and avoid confrontation. Therefore, they prefer an atmosphere that encourages close relationships, and achieve acceptance through conformity and loyalty.

They need to be appreciated, seek attention, and try to avoid confrontation. They want to be pleasant because they are irritated by insensitivity and impatience. They measure their personal worth by their degree of compatibility with others, and the depth of their relationships.

Under pressure, people who have this behavioural style will submit or acquiesce.

To influence and work with them, their managers need to support their feelings, and show how their ideas will support their personal circumstances.

Free Spirit style personalities appear to be more flamboyant. They have a tendency to interact within relationships and they dislike any loss of prestige. Their pace is fast and spontaneous. They try to create an atmosphere that encourages flexibility. They achieve acceptance through sociability and creating a stimulating environment.

They want to be admired, seek recognition, and dislike being ignored. They want you to be stimulating because they are irritated by routine and boredom. They measure their personal worth by the amount of recognition and acknowledgement (or complaints) they receive.

Under pressure, a free style behavioural type person will become offensive or sarcastic.

Team managers who want to be successful influencing and working with a person who uses this style will need to support their dreams and ideas and show how they can help enhance their standing with others.

Table 2 provides a quick reference for identifying these styles using body language.

Behavioural Style / Body Language	Driver, Controlling, Leadership Style	Analytical, Processing, or Task Style	People, Amiable, or Supporting Style	Free Spirit, Expressive, or Enthusing Style
Facial Expression	Fixed	Fixed	Varied	Varied
Eye Contact	Intense Long Duration	Reflective	Empathetic	Intense Short Duration, Scattered
Posture	Formal	Formal	Informal	Informal
Body Movement	Limited	Limited	More Mobility	More Mobility
Gestures Size Frequency	Small High	Small Low	Larger Low	Larger High
Voice Tone	Monotone	Monotone	Inflexion	Inflexion
Speed	Fast, Clipped	Slow, Measured	Slow, Measured	Fast
Volume/Force	Louder	Softer	Softer	Louder
Decision Making	Quick Limited Facts	Slower Lots of facts	Slower Lots of Opinions	Fast Intuition

Tips for Building Rapport with Driver, Controlling, or Leadership Style

Avoid:

- Wasting their time.
- Being vague and rambling.
- Getting too personal or try to get too close.
- Being disorganised.
- Straying from the purpose of the discussion.
- Asking irrelevant questions.
- Making wild claims.
- Trying to control the call.
- Trying to chitchat at length.

Try to achieve:

- Getting down to business quickly.
- Being specific in questioning.
- Efficient time use.
- Providing alternatives for them to choose from.
- Being factual and succinct.
- Talking about results and outcomes.
- Avoiding too much detail.

Tips for Building Rapport with Analytical, Processing, or Task Style

Avoid:

- Being disorganised and casual.
- Being late.
- Providing personal incentives.
- Pushing or coaxing.
- Using testimonials or options.

- Being flippant or gimmicky.

Try to achieve:

- Being well prepared.
- Getting straight down to business.
- Listening carefully.
- Being specific and logical.
- Being persistent and thorough when questioning.
- Being formal and unemotional when challenging.
- Giving them time to put in their point of view.

Tips for building rapport with People, Amiable, or Supporting Style

Avoid:

- Going straight into your discussion.
- Keeping the discussion subject focused all the time.
- Causing them to respond quickly.
- Dominating or controlling the discussion.
- Being rapid or abrupt.
- Keeping offering opinions or increasing the complexity of the decision.
- Making wild claims.
- Being very factual.

Try to achieve:

- Being friendly to show an interest in them personally.
- Being prepared for some chitchat before getting down to business.
- Taking time to uncover their needs by asking open questions.

- Being alert for non-verbal cues of dissatisfaction or disagreement.
- Being informal.
- Presenting your facts and points in a non-threatening way.
- Including guarantees and assurances wherever possible.
- Giving your presentation the personal touch.

Tips for Building Rapport with Free Spirit, Expressive, or Enthusing Style

Avoid:

- Controlling the discussion and keeping strictly to business.
- Being impatient.
- Inputting too much detail into the presentation.
- Tying them down there and then in making decisions.
- Socialising too much.
- Patronizing or digging your heels in.

Try to achieve:

- Some elements of socialising before the business.
- Talking about opinions and other people.
- Outline your ideas about what is being discussed.
- Being enthusiastic and energetic.
- Being fast paced.
- Offering incentives.

It is vital for the team manager who wants to coach effectively, to become skilled at building rapport quickly and easily. It is also vital that all team members are aware of their own and their team colleagues' styles.

7

Profile Your
Team's Strengths

I was a member of a team where the manager decided who was working on what project. There was no discussion. It was just a case of, "I want you to run this project". No discussion, and there was no point in challenging the decision as previous challenges had been totally ignored. Having said that, on this occasion (where the project did not sit with my specific strengths) I asked as to what the specific reasons were as to why they had decided on me running the project and not my colleague (who had the requisite strengths). In fact, given the complexity of the project it would have been great if the two of us had run the project jointly. This particular team manager did not like team members working jointly as "it was difficult to measure individual performance". As it turned out, their main reason for deciding on me running the project was to develop my weaknesses. In reality, it (allegedly) was probably a tactic to put me under pressure, as it was very possible that they were threatened by my greater experience and the fact that I did not flinch at challenging senior managers

– constructively of course! This managerial approach did not work, as working to develop weaknesses is nowhere near as effective as working on an individual's strengths. In this instance, the project did not quite go to plan as whilst there were elements of the project where I excelled, there were also elements where I struggled and was actually bored senseless! If we had gone with the partnership approach and worked on the project as a pair of colleagues with synergistic strengths, then it would have really worked well – for all involved.

It is a useful exercise to ensure that everyone in the team is fully aware of where their strengths lie, and this allows the team to ensure the right people are placed on the right projects. After all you would not put your rugby full back into a prop position or your football goalkeeper as your right winger!

I am indebted to Trudy Bateman, who is a Strengths Expert & Author and Head of Strengths Profiling at Cappfinity. Trudy has written this chapter where you will learn more about Strengths and their importance. Have a look at the Cappfinity website at www.cappfinity.com/. Trudy's book (co-authored with Alex Linley) entitled "The Strengths Profile Book" is also well worth a read.

The Benefits of Strengths

The science informs us that people perform better at work when using their strengths – and are a lot more engaged with what they are doing. People are happier when using their strengths, as well as feeling more capable and more confident in what they can achieve. Also, people grow, learn, and develop best in the areas of their strengths.

Businesses that invest in its employees' strengths and cultivate a strengths-based culture see an increase in sales, profit, and customer engagement. Here are five more reasons to be using strengths in your organisation.

1. **Tap into potential**
   If you are not using strengths, you are missing an opportunity to harness the potential and energy within your organisation. When people are working to their strengths, they are motivated and energised which has a direct result on productivity and financial performance. It's a win-win!

2. **Attract and retain**
   98% of people want their employers to recognise their strengths. Survey after survey has informed us that the companies who recognise and encourage their employees to work to their strengths are more attractive in the employment market and will also retain its employees for longer as they feel valued.

3. **Team transformation**
   When team managers are equipped to have strengths conversations with their team members, they increase their team's performance by 36%. Through focusing on collective strengths, tasks and projects are effectively delegated and volunteered for. Team members not only enjoy what they are working on, but also perform well at it.

4. **Supporting diversity**
   Diversity through recognising the uniqueness of our strengths is a great way to leverage the array of cultural backgrounds and life experiences within companies, as a strengths-based culture encourages people to value difference. Employers that authentically recognise the uniqueness of its employees' strengths have stronger teams,

collaborate effectively, and feel comfortable sharing ideas.

5. **Coping with change**
   The use of strengths broadens people's mindsets, encouraging new ways of thinking and acting, building resilience and the ability to bounce back. As I'm sure you know – the one constant in life is change!

What is a strength?

When people talk about strengths, we think about the things that you're good at. Cappfinity, the owners of Strengths Profile, define a strength through their research and years of 'strengthspotting' as having high Performance, Energy and Use.

Performance

For something to be a strength, you have to be good at it. This bit is likely to be the one thing you have already recognised in yourself through your life. You've probably been patted on the back a few times for achieving good results by doing this. However, performance alone is not enough to be a strength or to yield future success.

Energy

This is the most critical part. When you are using a strength, you feel energised. You feel motivated, you are enjoying using it and feel like you could go on all day. Knowing you are using a strength the next day makes you feel excited about getting up the next day. Strengths are deeply rewarding and fulfilling as they enable us to be our best self every day.

The third element of the Strengths Profile definition is use. If a strength isn't being used, we think this is something that needs some attention. If you perform well at something and enjoy it, but don't use it, you could be sitting on a potential talent to be utilised.

Strengths Profile assesses for 60 strengths and reveals 4 quadrants taking into consideration the results from your self-assessment on performance, energy and use. It reveals your realised strengths, unrealised strengths, learned behaviours and weaknesses.

How do you develop your Strengths?

Through the Strengths Profile Model of Development within each quadrant you will learn more about what you can do, can't do, and enjoy doing. You'll be able to use the language of strengths and develop yourself in all four categories to release your potential as per the advice below.

Realised Strengths – the things we perform well at, find energising, and use often – use wisely.

- Really understand them. Understand their stories, history, successes, and motivations.
- Align strengths to goals. To develop your strengths to best effect, you need to be clear on how they align to what you are doing now and also in the future.
- Use your strengths to compensate – for any impact that your learned behaviours or weaknesses have. For example, a weakness in Detail can be overcome through using a strength in Pride. Think about the strengths combinations that will work for your context.

- Don't overplay strengths – it's the right strength at the right time to the right amount. Strengths need to be turned up or down as appropriate for the situation. If not, you could get burned out and potentially annoy others.

Unrealised Strengths – things you perform well at, find energising but don't use often – use more

- Rank your unrealised strengths – Put them in order of preference for how much you would like to use each of them more. Concentrate on the top ones so you can further focus your efforts. There is no point trying to find an opportunity to use your unrealised strength of Detail more if you don't have the motivation.
- Gather any evidence – Consider a time you have used these strengths in the past. What was the outcome? Why was it enjoyable? What did you learn?
- Make a list of opportunities – No matter how small or unrealistic, how could you use your preferred unrealised strengths further? What does it look like to be more creative at work or be more adventurous at home?
- Use role models – Who do you think has this as a realised strength? What do they do and how do they do it? What can you learn from the way they get things done and collaborate with others?
- Go beyond your role – Volunteer for extra activities outside of your natural role to show interest and gain experience. For example, if you want to share your Writer strength, produce some internal communications or guidelines in your area of expertise.

Learned Behaviours – things we perform well at but find de-energising – use when needed.

Using your learned behaviours will give you performance but not energy and this often leads to lightbulb moments in coaching. Learned behaviours aren't bad; after all, they are things that we do well. It's just that they are de-energising over time. To be at your best over the long-term, you need to use your learned behaviours as needed rather than relying on them all the time.

- Refocus the role – Reorganise your activities in a way that reduces the extent to which you have to use a particular learned behaviour. In doing so you will ideally play more to your realised and unrealised strengths.
- Timing: organise tasks into 'strengths sandwiches' – be more mindful of how and when you complete less energising activities. Try to create a better balance by sandwiching activities that drain you between more energising activities that play to your strengths.
- Find a complementary partner – work with someone who would be energised by taking on the things that you get drained by. In return, do something for them that they struggle with, which will help performance for both of you to be sustainable over time.

Weaknesses – things we don't perform well at and find de-energising – use less.

We need to know what our weaknesses are, and then manage them in a way that minimises them and makes their impact irrelevant. Here is how to use your weaknesses less and minimise their impact:

- Reshape your approach – when a task requires you to use a weakness, consider achieving it by using a different strength. What if you viewed the task as not making small talk so using your weakness of Rapport Builder, but instead you tasked yourself with finding out more about something of interest about the person using your strength of Curiosity.
- Use strengths to compensate – Can you use or apply one or more of your strengths in such a way that your weakness is compensated for? For example, a strength in Resilience might enable you to overcome a weakness in Feedback.
- Adopt strengths-based team working – work more using a 'team strengths' approach. Lean on your team members more by allocating tasks, objectives, or responsibilities according to the strengths of people.

Applying my Strengths

Individually – Strengths use increases confidence, well-being, and resilience so it's all about finding new ways to use your strengths. Use the tips in your Strengths Profile for practical advice. Make your strengths visible, share them and volunteer for areas that will develop them further.

At work – encourage strengths-based team working and give feedback based on strengths you see in action. Recognise and celebrate your colleagues' strengths (and weaknesses) so you know how you can support each other to be more effective. Team up in pairs for a powerful result when you share strengths and complement each other where you are different.

Share your Profile with your manager and encourage future career conversations. Set goals according to your strengths and use strengths to fine-tune your role. Identify ways you can use an unrealised strength that you are passionate about developing.

In your teams – strength-spot. Develop your colleagues further by helping them to understand their strengths use. Use this intelligence to help people work on the right things at the right time. Pay attention to energy from your team members, and what gets done and what always seems to slip. When are your colleagues most energised and engaged at work?

When you observe one of your colleagues using a strength, tell them! Explain the positive impact it had on the situation in real time to encourage further use. Don't be tempted with just saying "that's great".

Help colleagues and team members overcome any business-critical weaknesses that could impact the team or the team goals. Consider how they might overcome these with their strengths or see who else in the team has this as a strength that might be able to support them.

Team meetings are a great opportunity to understand the team dynamics and reflect on how you can leverage the collective strengths. Pay attention to who will speak up verses who will need to reflect on decisions. Who is likely to take action or consider the impact?

Encourage everyone to share their learning, goals, and dreams with colleagues and managers. This could be during formal or informal conversations, but it will give people a chance to spot opportunities for others.

As a Parent – encourage them to know themselves. Talk

about strengths at home. Pick up on subtle clues about their day that can open an opportunity to reinforce a strength, or to recognise things that they may simply not be so good at – and reassure them that this is OK. When you do see that spark of greatness in your child, try planting a 'golden seed' – a kind word, a hug, reinforcement, encouragement, or positive feedback.

Strengthening Managers – If you want outstanding performance and engaged happy workers, identify your team members' strengths. Get to know your own strengths. Share your own strengths stories with your team and understand how you are different or similar to each team member. Help your team members to harness their strengths in delivering your team objectives and corporate strategy. Use the Strengths Profile Team Manager Profile and Manager Toolkit to learn more about strengths-based management. It's full of tips on how to bring strengths more into your management conversations and daily meetings.

Strengthening your Career – Find careers that match your strengths so you can turn up every day at work and enjoy what you do. The Strengths Profile Career Guide, included in the Profile will support you to:

- Look at where the focus needs to be today, next year and next decade.
- Know job sector suggestions to support career conversations around where to take that potential next step.
- Have focused encouragement on the types of careers in the right sector to research, helping to maximise potential.
- Be able to confident in career transitioning.

- Take on the right job rotations and job sharing through aligning strengths and motivations for success.
- Strategically leveraging our career networks to find out more about the job sectors.

Balancing the Mix

With regards to teams, the team manager should always where possible try to get the right mix of both personalities, strengths, and skills within the team. A lot of the time this is not possible, especially where a manager takes on a team that is already formed and established. In this case the manager has a challenge whereby if there are any gaps in either personality, strengths, or skills, he or she must endeavour to fill these gaps. I have found the two models already discussed (Behavioural Styles & Strengths) useful in assessing the mix of the team but you could also use a third model which is the Meredith Belbin Model of Team Roles which is covered (top-line) in the next chapter.

If we first look at Behavioural Styles, ideally you would want to have a team that was a mixture of all four styles. i.e., Driver to add focus and assertion; Analyst to add method, structure, and quality; Expressive to add creativity, energy, and innovation and Amiable to add diplomacy and harmony. An imbalance can lead to the team manager having to firstly identify the gap and then fill the gap by adapting his or her own behavioural style to reinstate the balance. Looking at extremes. If you have a team of four individuals and everyone has the same behavioural style you might experience the following:

All Drivers: You would certainly get focus and a drive to get results. However, given that drivers usually think that their way is best, you may get some serious conflict as people try to get their own way. Also, there may be a lack of creativity and quality about their work.

All Analysts: There will be plenty of quality and structure here but as with the drivers, there may be a lack of creativity and energy and this in turn may mean that the task takes ages to be completed, if at all!

All Amiable: Loads of harmony and together-ness with a degree of creativity although this group will always look for reassurance and support. They will need to ask for advice and opinions from senior management. There may be a distinct lack of risk taking and again they may take far too long to complete the task.

All Expressive: An all-expressive team has loads of energy, ideas and will take risks but the team will have little structure, quality, and method. The team may be error prone and may end up completing projects but with a different and possibly wrong result!

Getting the right balance of styles can pay big dividends if you are looking for the team to function well but the team manager will have to be a good facilitator and coach as having the right mix means different styles working together and there is always the tendency for the styles to clash.

8

The Belbin Team
Roles Model

Another model, which can be useful, is Meredith Belbin's Team Roles Model, an outline of which is below. This is another team-building' exercise that can be undertaken to raise awareness of the individual team members' personalities and strengths and Belbin's model looks specifically at the various 'roles' that individual team members prefer to take within group and team situations. It is useful to overlay this model with the Strengths Profile of each individual to really confirm that you have the right mix of team members when having them work together on projects.

BELBIN'S TEAM ROLES

(adapted from Belbin, 1981)

ROLE	OBSERVED CONTRIBUTIONS
CHAIRPERSON:	Clarifying the goals and objectives of the group.
	Selecting the problems on which decisions have to be made and establishing their priorities.
	Helping establish roles, responsibilities, and work boundaries within the group.
	Summing up the feelings and achievements of the group, and articulating group verdicts.
SHAPER:	Shaping roles, boundaries, responsibilities, tasks, and objectives.
	Finding or seeking to find pattern m group discussion.
	Pushing the group towards agreement on policy and action and towards making decisions.
PLANT:	Advancing proposals.
	Making criticisms that lead up to counter-suggestions.
	Offering new insights *on* lines of action already agreed.
MONITOR/ EVALUATOR:	Analysing problems and situations.
	Interpreting complex written material and clarifying obscurities.
	Assessing the judgements and contributions of others.

COMPANY WORKER: Transforming talk and ideas into practical steps.

Considering what is feasible.

Trimming suggestions to make them fit into agreed plans and established systems.

TEAM WORKER: Giving personal support and help to others.

Building on to or seconding a member's ideas and suggestions.

Drawing the reticent into discussion.

Taking steps to avert or overcome disruption of the team.

RESOURCE INVESTIGATOR: Introducing ideas and developments of external origin.

Contacting other individuals or groups of own volition.

Engaging in negotiation-type activities.

COMPLETER: Emphasizing the need for task completion, meeting W" and schedules and generally promoting a sense of urgency.

Looking for and spotting errors, omissions, and oversights.

Galvanizing others into activity.

SPECIALIST: Single minded self -tarting & dedicated Provides specialist knowledge and skills.

By utilising the models above the team manager can help raise awareness of the team's strengths and weaknesses and ensure that the right approach is taking to developing the team further. Like the other models, you can do an online questionnaire for Belbin which will produce a report for your team. Check out www.belbin.com

9

Team Meetings and Reviews - Physical and Virtual

Team managers and teams spend probably too much time in meetings, (both physical and virtual) but team meetings can (and should be) a fantastic medium in which to coach and develop the team towards high performance. Provided the meeting is for a useful purpose (and amazingly a good number are not!) then the team manager can use this opportunity to use their coaching skills to great effect and to support the team to improve cohesiveness and performance. The following are some pointers as to how the team manager and the team, can make the most productive use of team meetings.

The Physical Meeting:

1. Why is the team meeting being called? Make sure it is for a distinct purpose with measurable objectives and specific outcomes. There is nothing worse than calling a team meeting with little

substance just because it is the norm. I have been to many sales review meetings, which were held every month because that it what has always been done. Only call the team meeting if it is necessary!

2. As a team manager you will have outcomes based on your agenda items, but will they take up the whole time? Ask the team what they would like to see on the agenda and get team members to take responsibility for running their own session or topic. Make sure they have practical outcomes. High performing teams share the leadership of team meetings so that it does not always have to be the team manager who organises the meeting and facilitates the meeting. Sharing the tasks involved in team meetings builds skills, knowledge, and the accountability of all team members. I repeat this message later in this chapter as it is a real feature of high-performance teams!

3. Once the agenda is compiled make sure that each agenda item has a desired outcome, and that this outcome will be achieved through an agreed process. It helps to vary the process for different agenda items where possible. Use presentation, group discussion, business case scenarios, problem solving sessions, role-play, expert presenters, etc to make team meetings varied and enjoyable. Sitting through a full day team meeting where the team manager hogs the stage and presents back 'death by power-point' all the time does not make for a productive and motivational team meeting! This is even more painful when the team meeting is held virtually!

4. Communicate the agenda outlining to the team what specific topics are to be discussed, what processes are to be used, and what the outcomes are for each topic. If there is any preparation work to be done ensure that each team member knows what they must do and what they must bring with them. Ensure each agenda topic has a timescale and it is probably best to prioritise the topics in relation to importance and urgency to the business.

5. Before the team meeting starts, remind the team of the "ground rules" that you have agreed as a team for meetings. Also, it useful to have a 'minute' or 'actions taker' and a timekeeper to ensure the team meeting process goes smoothly.

6. Check the "mood" of the team before the team meeting takes place. Has anything cropped up that may have an affect of the team and potentially the previously agreed agenda? If the group's minds are elsewhere then you may not achieve your meeting's outcomes. I remember a sales meeting many years ago where the manager insisted that we go through the agreed agenda (his!) even though the company, only the day before had issued a profits warning and hinted that there may be redundancies. Was anyone really interested at that point in time about last month's sales report and activity figures? No! Flex your agenda to address fears and concerns first before moving the team meeting on. Otherwise, your level of engagement will be negligible and possibly non-existent!

7. Ensure participation from each team member

where appropriate. It is important that all team members feel "included", that they have a degree of "control" and that people are thanked for their contributions ("affection"). Again, remind yourself of the ICA model of teams by referring to a previous chapter.

8. Continually check the process and mood of the team as the team meeting progresses. Is the process working for them and is the meeting on track to achieve its aims? If not, be flexible; adapt either the process or agenda or both.

9. Make sure there are adequate breaks for teas/coffees/lunch. Do not try to cram an agenda.

10. Where possible (and be disciplined in this!), build in development time for the team. Can you use some team meeting time to deliver aspects of your team development plan or review progress of development plan for the team? People feel great if they leave team meetings having fulfilled their agenda outcomes and have learned something new that they can take away to support their roles.

11. On the development side ensure you give team members the chance to develop their team meeting skills such as team meeting organisation, coaching and facilitation. As the team manager do you always have to organise and run the team meeting? No – develop your team's individual members to take on such tasks periodically! And make sure you coach and direct them appropriately when they take on such developmental tasks so as

to give them the necessary support to deliver. Do not dump the tasks on them without giving them support. Otherwise, your team meeting may not go as well as you would have hoped for!

12. Make sure all the main discussion points and actions are documented and circulated so as you can follow up on progress with each topic.

13. Get feedback from the team as to how the team meeting went and how it was for them personally. Did you achieve the team meeting's objectives? What went well? What not so well? What do you have to do next time to make your next team meeting even better?

Team meetings are a chance for you as a team manager, to communicate to, listen to, inspire, and develop your team and the individuals within it. Although not all team meetings called can achieve this, if you as a team manager are in control you can ensure that your team meetings go well, and that all team members look forward to them if you follow the above principles. Now a tale to reinforce the above points.

The Weekly Review Meeting – A Tale of Two Teams

This is the tale of two teams who had embarked on weekly team 'get togethers' and one which highlights the major differences in outputs, team morale and enthusiasm in relation to how these meetings were run.

Let us look at the first team. This was a specialist sales team of four members who had recently gained a new team manager. The previous team manager had held informal weekly chats with each team member and held virtual team meetings every month with a full 'physical' team meeting every quarter. This was how the team reviews had run historically. The new team manager came in and moved the team meetings to being completely virtual to save time and money as well as implementing a weekly 'project and objectives review' meeting. This team meeting would give the team members the opportunity over 15 minutes to run through how their projects were progressing outlining the completed actions and successes from the previous week along with the specific actions that were to be put in the place for the week ahead. This was to be held at 8am every Monday morning by Skype. A project and objectives planner was put in place and each team member updated the planner at the end of each week. This, in business terms, is best practice for many teams, but for this team it was a real departure from what they were normally used to. Little explanation was given by the new team manager apart from a 'it will keep you on track' comment. Asked if the 8am was negotiable the reply was that this was the best time to have these as it meant everyone was ready to go for the week. No flexibility was given.

Expecting the new team manager to take the lead and share their own projects and objectives, the team were surprised to find that the new team manager expected everyone to report back within their allocated 15 minutes but there was no time allocation for the new team manager. This was not how the previous manager had operated and very quickly distrust and suspicion started to rise within the team. Whereas the previous team manager had consulted with the team around agendas and processes and had also shared the chairing of team meetings around the team, this new manager constructed the agenda and chaired the meetings. The weekly team catch-up which should have been looked forward to in terms of sharing successes and hearing about others' progress, quickly became demotivational with the team members feeling that they were distrusted and were constantly being 'watched'. The team meeting felt like a 'justification of your role' meeting and as each week went past, more people started to call off due to having an early 'appointment' or would pull out of the team meeting due to 'internet' issues. The team meetings also became farcical as the new team manager would turn up late for some meetings but still expected the same outputs. And there was still no update on the new team manager's projects or objectives. Some team members eventually 'moved on' not solely because of these team meetings, but they did play an important part in those team member's decisions.

Let us contrast this with another weekly team meeting. The setting this time is a distribution company and the team (6 members) is warehouse based where all the team meetings are physical, so the virtual dynamic does not come into play. However, the actions and behaviours of the team manager compared to the sales team manager are worthy of mention. This warehouse also had a new team manager and an inexperienced team manager to boot. However, this team manager consulted with the team about how previous weekly team meetings were run and they established what had worked well and perhaps needed changed moving forward. The aims and the format of the weekly team meeting were also a team decision. Times of starting were agreed at 9am each Monday morning but the start time could be flexible to ensure that by the team meeting start time everyone was settled and had handled any urgent requests and were fully prepared with a coffee. The new team manager led the way. The team manager outlined their individual outputs from the previous week and what they were working on in the week ahead. The team followed suit and there was a real feeling of 'togetherness'. After each team meeting there was a summary of any agreed team actions and a quick review as to how each person felt the meeting had gone. There was also agreement as to who was going to lead and facilitate the next team meeting so that everyone got the chance to develop their leadership and chairing skills. Observing this team in action was a joy to behold!

So, what can we learn from this 'tale of two teams'?

- If you are a new team manager make sure you hold that vital 'getting to know you' and 'contracting' team meeting!
- Weekly review team meetings are good and when run effectively can lead to a real team 'togetherness' as well as improved focus, productivity, sharing of learning, problem solving and celebration of success.
- Successes can be shared and celebrated, and challenges outlined, with solutions suggested through the support of the team.
- Team managers and leaders should show proper leadership and involve the team in the structure and running of the team meetings.
- Team managers and leaders should 'model the way' by sharing their objectives, actions, successes, and challenges.
- Shared leadership of the team meetings is a real opportunity to develop the team members and embed real 'team ownership'.

As a team manager or team leader – how motivational and productive are your team review meetings?

What about the Virtual Team Meeting?

Virtual team meetings have now become commonplace in the professional workplace, allowing for a face-to-face experience that can serve as a viable substitute for the 'real' thing. Many international teams have used video conferencing routinely in the past, so it is not a new phenomenon. However, with recent events surrounding the COVID-19 pandemic, many businesses now find themselves dependent on virtual meetings to conduct business, keep projects moving forward and communicate with remote teams and clients. And while nothing can fully replace the physical meeting, taking the right virtual approach can ensure a successful outcome.

Below are 10 tips for running a great virtual team meeting whether it is via Zoom, Microsoft Teams, Blue Jeans etc.

1. **Use a solid and reliable video conference / virtual platform and ensure you put the time in to ensure the whole team learn how to use it effectively and work out technical glitches before any virtual team meeting.**

Every virtual team meeting requires technology to make it possible. And there are numerous video conferencing solutions available today, with Zoom, GoToMeeting, Microsoft Teams, Skype, Blue Jeans and WebEx being just a few of the most popular. Most solutions share a similar feature set, with subtle differences in their options and interface. The important aspect is that the team should be fully proficient in the use of the platform remembering that it is not just the internal team meetings that this medium will be used in – it is also for customer meetings as well!

2. **Make sure the Team agrees to a Mandatory Video-on Policy.**

Virtual meetings are far better when everyone's video cameras are being used. One of your goals should be to make virtual team meetings feel as much like an in-person meeting as possible. So being able to see the other people "in the meeting" plays an important role in maximising communication and ensuring full engagement. Communication is simply more effective when non-verbal clues can be picked up on and when faces are visible and facial expressions and body language are on display. All team members (unless a client declined your request) should have their camera on for every virtual team meeting and each participant should sit close to their laptop or webcam to simulate the intimacy of an in-person meeting. Do not be like the team manager I had experience of who never put their camera on despite feedback!

Make virtual team meetings feel as much like an in-person meeting as possible.

3.   Face-to-face Team Meeting etiquette is Virtual Team Meeting etiquette.

One of the most important rules to follow for virtual team meetings is to make sure everyone follows face-to-face meeting etiquette even though you are in a virtual environment. In other words, if it is not acceptable in a physical team meeting, it should not be acceptable in a virtual team meeting.

a. Unless it is a working team lunch, you really should not be eating food although I would suggest that a coffee, tea, or a drink is acceptable.

b. Team members should not get up and walk around the room unless it is a 'team stretch'.

c. Everyone should stay engaged and if the engagement in the team meeting is waning, then this should be fed back to the team by any individual concerned. Members of high-performance teams will be confident to do this, members of Pseudo teams may not be!

d. Do not have the mobile on and do not take phone calls.

e. Turn off audible notifications from email and text
    messages.

Everyone's approach to a virtual team meeting should be the
same approach to a physical team meeting.

4.   Discourage Multi-tasking.
Multi-tasking should not be allowed or tolerated as being fully
engaged is crucial to a great team meeting, so all attendees
should be singularly focused on the meeting at hand, not
responding to emails or text messages. While there is great
temptation to multi-task during a virtual team meeting, the
rules of engagement should be respected and enforced. In fact,
research shows that multi-tasking harms your performance
and negatively impacts the effectiveness of a virtual team
meeting. There is also nothing worse than when a good team
manager or facilitator knows when you are multi-tasking and
then expertly asks you a direct question about what is being
discussed or presented. Potential embarrassment awaits!

**5.   Include Everyone in the Virtual Room where
       possible!**
Just as everyone is greeted by name as they join a physical
team meeting, the same should apply in a virtual environment.
It may seem like an insignificant thing, but simply saying hello
and acknowledging every participant by name will do wonders
to enhance collaboration, unity, and team meeting success. If
there are participants that do not know one another, brief
introductions are essential to get the meeting started off right.
Remember the key ICA model for team inclusion presented
earlier in this book!

6.   Make the Team Meeting Interactive.
While this is true of physical team meetings as well, virtual

team meetings by nature can be dominated by the more domineering personalities and the extroverts on the call. It is easier to shrink back in a virtual team meeting and take a 'back seat' so Team meeting leaders should not allow this to occur and should involve every team member where practical. Every team member has a voice and it the duty of those running the team meeting to get everyone involved.

So, what are some ways to get the quieter, more introverted participants involved? It starts by intentionally seeking out their input and giving them "screen time" by asking them probing questions that allow the opportunity for their voice to be heard. Here are some questions to consider asking:

- Ask for their opinions on specific tasks/projects— even if they are not part of the project team.
- Ask for quick updates about their priorities, challenges, successes, etc.
- Ask if they have anything to add to viewpoints that have already been shared by others
- Ask if they need any help with their workload or if they have capacity to give.

You can also make available various 'interactive' apps such as Mentimeter and WePollanywhere. Zoom and Microsoft Teams have Breakout Rooms and Whiteboards so team managers and facilitators should get upskilled in using these to ensure interactivity in team meetings within the virtual meeting space.

7.   Focus on the real Priorities.

As in physical team meetings, every virtual team meeting should have an agenda and a clear objective. Be sensitive to everyone's time and cognisant of the abundance of virtual meetings that are taking place throughout the day. Stick to the agenda, avoid 'curve-balls', and take minor issues and other conversations that do not impact the entire group, offline.

Every virtual team meeting should have an agenda, clear objectives, and detailed outcome focused topics.

8.   Keep Sessions, Short and Focused.
With the sheer abundance of virtual meetings taking place these days, keeping these team meetings as short and efficient as possible should be an objective. It is best to try to keep your meetings at one hour or less, ideally between 15 to 45 minutes to make optimum use of the time and so that every participant can stay focused. If an hour or less is not sufficient to cover all that you need to cover, consider breaking the team meeting up into two separate meetings or plan a 15-minute "break" to allow your team a chance to get up and stretch, respond to emails and or personal things that may be required of them. Long meetings—especially virtual meetings—provide challenges for participants to stay focused and not become bored or lose interest. Short and focused meetings are the recipe for increased productivity and meeting success. The phenomenon known as 'Zoom Fatigue' is very real and it is amazing how many organisations are ignoring the advice to keep virtual team meetings limited and to ensure short agenda items and allow decent breaks. The 'back-to-back' meeting culture is unfortunately 'alive and kicking' and to be honest this needs to be challenged and 'kicked into touch'.

9.   Do you really need a virtual team meeting? Or will a conference call via the mobile do?
There are now possibly too many virtual meetings taking place throughout the day for every one of your staff, partners, and clients, which can lead to screen fatigue. While regular communication and video "face time" is necessary in a virtual work environment, it is also important to stop and

consider in each instance whether a virtual team meeting is required. Over-communicating can be as unhelpful as under communicating. We need to make sure that we allow people the space to get deep work done and focus on the tasks at hand.

10. **Adapt to the 'idiosyncrasies' of virtual team meetings and develop the skills of the team.**

While virtual business and team meetings share similarities to their physical counterparts, it is important to identify and adapt to the differences. A great virtual team meeting does not happen without preparation and effort. As the saying goes, 'practice makes perfect' so it is important that all the team members are as skilled as the team manager or leader. After all, if you are to be a high-performance team then shared leadership should be the norm.

10

Managing Team Conflict and Under Performance

A major advantage a team has over an individual is its diversity of resources, combined knowledge, and ideas and providing these are all accessed and 'pooled' together then the team can be a far more impactful and productive force than simply individuals operating alone. However, diversity also produces conflict. As more and more organisations restructure and 're-set' because of COVID-19 to create and 'refresh' teams, the need for teams to be skilled in managing conflict productively will grow. It is critical that team managers and leaders possess these skills in order that conflict is minimised, resolved and that their teams grow as a result.

Conflict arises from differences. When individuals come together in teams their differences in terms of behavioural styles, intangible needs, values, physical needs, expectations, attitudes, behaviours, and social factors all contribute to the creation of conflict. It is often difficult to fully expose the sources of conflict as this can arise from numerous sources within a team setting. Generally, though, it falls into three categories: communication factors, structural factors, and personal factors.

Barriers to communication are among the most important factors and can be a major source of misunderstanding. Communication barriers include poor team leadership, inadequate listening skills; insufficient sharing of information; differences in interpretation and perception; and nonverbal cues being ignored or missed.

Structural disagreements include the size of the organisation, company strategy, turnover rate, levels of participation, reward systems, and differing levels of interdependence among employees. Inadequately structured teams can also contribute to this and those pseudo and potential teams devoid of team contracts or charters can fall prey to situations where conflict arises very quickly.

Personal factors include things such as an individual's personal circumstances, their personal goals, values, expectations, situations and needs.

For conflict to be dealt with successfully, team managers and team members must understand its unpredictability and its impact on individuals and the team.

Conflict in work teams is not necessarily destructive, however, and conflict can lead to new ideas and approaches. Conflict, in this sense, can be considered positive, as it facilitates the surfacing of important issues and provides opportunities for people to develop their communication and interpersonal skills. Conflict becomes negative when it is left to escalate to the point where people begin to feel defeated, and a combative climate of distrust and suspicion develops. Team members can and should attempt to avoid negative conflict from occurring and the best way to prevent negative conflict is to ensure that a solid team contract is created by the team and reviewed routinely by the team. Time should be put aside for the team to create the contract and real focus should be placed on having an open and honest discussion about team purpose, its aims and goals, roles and responsibilities, individual needs, and expectations as well as decision making and empowerment processes. Have you heard this before in this book?

Handling Negative Conflict

When negative conflict does occur, there are five accepted methods for handling it: Direct Approach, Bargaining, Enforcement, Retreat, and De-emphasis. Each can be used effectively in different circumstances.

1. **Direct Approach:** This may be the best approach of all. It concentrates on the team manager confronting the issue head-on. In high performance or self-directed teams individual team members tackle it head on without relying on the team manager or leader. Although conflict can be uncomfortable to deal with, it is best to look at issues objectively and to face them as they are. If criticism is used, it must be constructive to the recipients. This approach counts on the techniques of problem-solving and normally leaves everyone with a sense of resolution, because issues are brought to the surface and dealt with. Above all it requires an openness, an awareness, and a positive solutions-focused mindset from all team members. If the organisation possesses a 'blame' culture, then it will not happen.

2. **Bargaining:** This is an excellent technique when team members have ideas on a solution yet cannot find common ground. Often a third party, such as a team manager or team leader, is needed to help find the compromise. Compromise involves give and take on both sides, however, and can end up with both walking away equally dissatisfied so care must be taken here.

3. **Enforcement of Team Contract, Agreement or Rules:** Whilst the creation of a team contract is an essential 'building block' to ensure the progress to high performance, the actual 'enforcement' of the contract is only used when it is obvious that a team member does not want to be a team player and refuses to work with the rest of the team. The Team Contract should be reviewed proactively to ensure that all agreements are working for the team, but a reactive enforcement of the contract should be avoided if at all possible. If enforcement must be used on an individual team member, it may be best for that person to find another team.

4. **Retreat:** Only use this method when the problem is not real to begin with. By simply avoiding it or working around it, a team manager or team leader can often delay long enough for the individual team member to cool off or the issue to fade away. When used in the right environment by an experienced team manager this technique can help to prevent minor incidents that are the result of someone simply having a bad day.

5. **De-emphasis:** This is a form of bargaining where

the emphasis is on the areas of agreement. When parties realise that there are areas where they agree, they can often begin to move in a new direction. It may be useful though, despite the overall agreement that any conflict is discussed openly so that it does not re-emerge or escalate in he future. In other words, do not ignore it simply because there is an overall agreement.

Team Resolution Process

If conflict has got to the stage where it needs further investigation and resolution, and involves specific individual team members, then further action may be needed.

Conflict should first be handled on an informal basis between the individuals involved. This will allow time for resolution or self- correction by the individuals. If the conflict remains unsettled via the team manager, a mediator can be brought in to help resolve the situation. If resolution is still not achieved the dispute should be openly discussed in a team meeting. A formal discipline process needs to occur if resolution is not achieved after being addressed at the team level. The escalating process of Team Resolution is as follows:

1. **Collaboration (One-on-one):** Handle the new problem person-to-person. Use as many facts as possible and relate the issue to customer, team, or organisational needs. Be open and honest and conduct the session in a private setting. Document the concerns or issues, the dates, and the resolution, if any, and have both parties sign it.

2. **Mediation (One-on-one with Mediator):** If collaboration did not work or was inappropriate,

handle the problem with a mediator. The mediator must be trained in conflict resolution, understand policy and ethics, be trusted by the team, and can remain neutral. Gather facts and talk over the issue with the people involved. Bring up as many facts as possible and relate the issue to customer, team, or organisational needs. Be open and honest and conduct the mediation session in private. Document it and have all those involved, sign what was agreed.

3. **Team Counselling:** If the conflict is a definite issue for the team and collaboration and/or mediation could not be done, were not appropriate, or did not work, then handle the conflict at a team meeting. Put the problem on the next agenda and invite the necessary individuals. Again, bring up the facts, relate the issue to customer, team, or organisational needs. Be open and honest, discuss it in a private setting, document it, and have all parties sign it. Anyone on the team can put an issue or problem on the team agenda, however, this step should be used only after Collaboration, and Mediation has been ruled out.

Managing Cooperative Conflict

Though we often view conflict through a negative lens, teams require some conflict to operate effectively. Cooperative conflict can contribute to effective problem solving and decision making by motivating people to examine a problem. By encouraging the expression of many ideas, energising people to seek a superior solution, and fostering integration of several ideas then high-quality solutions can be created.

The key to managing conflict is to understand how to handle it constructively. If team members understand how to manage it, then they are more liable to feel confident in raising issues and putting forward ideas. This way, healthy 'debate' can ensue. To build an environment where 'healthy debate' is the norm then the starting point to building trust and confidence is the creation of the team contract.

While it is true that suppressed differences can reduce the effectiveness of a team, when they are brought to the surface, disagreements can be dealt with and problems can be resolved. The actual process of airing differences can help to increase the cohesiveness and effectiveness of the team through the increased interest and energy that often accompanies it. This in turn fosters creativity and intensity among team members. In addition, bringing differences to the surface can result in better ideas and more innovative solutions. When people share their views and strive toward reaching a consensus, better decisions are reached. Team members also improve their communication skills and become better at understanding and listening to the information they receive when differences are freely aired.

For individuals to work effectively in teams they must be able to clearly communicate their ideas, to listen, and be willing to disagree. Although it is difficult, learning to appreciate each other's differences reflects a team's ability to manage conflict. When conflict occurs, we must not turn our backs and hope it will go away. Instead, we must learn to tolerate it, even welcome it, for well-managed conflict can be the source of change and innovation.

As more and more organisations attempt to make the difficult transition to increase their teamwork or 'refresh' their current teams they must develop and provide programmes for their employees which offer training in team conflict management skills and techniques. Above all, prevention is better than cure, and having the skills and expertise in creating effective and impactful team contracts and agreements is an absolute must.

Dealing with Disruptives

Keeping on the 'conflict' front, whilst conflict can simply be caused by differences in personality styles and other 'team' factors such as a lack of clarity and understanding of situations, these can usually be remedied by raising awareness with behavioural styles training, strengths profiling and a solidly constructed team charter.

However, there may be some team members who cause conflict due to their specific behaviours and attitudes. Below I will outline some types of individuals who may have to be handled carefully and correctly, for team conflict to be minimised.

The "Prima Donna" – These people tend to be talented and tend to let people know about it! They think that because of their talent they do not have to abide by the team's agreed rules or contract, and they demand that the other team members attend to them, while they themselves ignore the needs of the team. Even when the team do try to include the "prima donna" they are brushed off. The "prima donna" oozes arrogance. How does the team manager (or team if a high-performance team) handle this type of person?

Firstly, recognise that their personality is not their fault and secondly, appreciate that what you see is not all there is. Arrogant people often have major insecurities and may be experiencing more pain and stress than the other team members. There may also be stresses out with the workplace so be prepared to perhaps at some point to become the "counselling" team manager or if you are not qualified in that area, to refer onwards. Thirdly, just check that the team itself is not causing the problem. Sometimes the "prima donna's" arrogance is due to being excluded from the team as the team find it hard to deal with the "Prima Donna's" extra talent and to that end start to exclude them deliberately. Also check that your team rules are not so strict that they are preventing creativity and innovation.

The behaviour of the "Prima Donna" must be highlighted to the "Prima Donna" themselves and the team manager should ensure that not only is the feedback given constructively but a "listening ear" is given as to why the behaviour is occurring. Only then can a meaningful discussion take place as to how best to move forward in order that the disruptive behaviours are replaced with productive ones along with the scope for the "Prima Donna" to remain at their creative best. It may be useful to consider giving them a "specialist" role within the team and make sure that you keep reviewing their progress with them regularly and do not forget the recognition of their efforts!

The "Dominator" – Every team has them – a person who always wants to dominate team activities and ensure they get the lion's share of attention. The usual way of dealing with the dominator is to "slap them down" by either telling them outright to quit their domineering behaviours or by both ignoring and talking over them, or by relegating them to tasks out with the team. I believe this is counter-productive and it is in these situations where the team manager comes to the fore in team meetings. How about the following?

a. Call on the other team members to contribute. When the "dominator" pipes up acknowledge their contribution and encourage the other team members to come up with their own contributions.

b. Make the team agenda work by sticking to it. Many "dominators" will throw in "wobblies" or 'curve balls' that take the team away from the agenda. The team manager should ensure that tangents do not happen and skilfully bring the meeting back on course.

c. When the "dominator" throws in an idea or a suggestion then the team manager should probe as to what is behind the suggestion, how it fits with the agenda, and what desired outcomes they desire. The team manager can then ask the team for their comments and thoughts on it. Do not agree with the dominator before the other contributions!

d. If the "dominator" continues to attempt to control the meeting, then at the next break take them aside and give them the constructive feedback that they deserve! They must be told of the negative impact of their interventions.

The "You Owe Me" Individuals – These people think that the company they work for owes them in terms of a job, a decent wage, and good working conditions. In many ways they act like "spoilt brats" and expect everything to be done for them. They take a negative approach and will complain at the slightest change in company policy. Examples include the company car policy, lunch allowances, pensions, entertainment budgets and holiday entitlements. This has resulted, in many cases, due to people becoming too comfortable because of reduced responsibility. In other words, it is due to bad or mediocre performance management by team managers themselves!

The team manager can handle the "you owe mes" through vigilance and intolerance. Vigilance, by closely monitoring performance against agreed performance objectives and intolerance in terms of ensuring that these objectives are not so easily achievable that the person is not stretched. Too often team members get by by doing the minimum when really, they should have to work to hit objectives. Only by having stretching objectives will they ever perform at the highest level. Rewards that are given must be for achievement and not for simply "turning up".

The "Saboteur" – There will be on occasion times when the team manager will have to deal with the "saboteur". This is the team member who tells you one thing and then does another. Or tells the team one thing and then tells you another. They are out to split the team and perhaps create a division between the team manager and the rest of the team. Sometimes they can pick on individuals. Perhaps they see these individuals as a threat and as such start to spread rumours about them, or worse, sneak to the boss to tell them when the person has made a mistake. Even worse than that is to tell lies about them or about what they have done or not done!

There is only one way to deal with "saboteurs". Firstly, establish exactly what the truth is. Once this is established and that you are 100% certain in your facts, and that you have found out that the "saboteur" has been at work, then confront them and start the disciplinary process. Sounds harsh? It is and deserves to be. Teams cannot sustain saboteurs and the saboteur must know how destructive their behaviours are. They also must know what the consequences of their behaviours are in relation to the team. This sort of behaviour cannot be tolerated.

A Final word about Handling Performance

This is not a management handbook and as such I am not going into too much detail about how best to handle performance or specifically under-performance. There are though, a few guidelines for teams to consider when underperformance is a challenge for the team.

1. **Identify exactly what the under-performance is?** This should be straightforward as the team should have a business plan, a team contract, and a team development plan. In other words, the support frameworks are in place and within the specific objectives, particularly within the business plan, the under-performance will be linked to one or more business objectives.

2. **Analyse the specific nature of the under-performance** by gathering as much data and information from the team as is possible so that the root-cause of the under-performance can be identified. Get the team into the way of regularly problem solving but ensuring that the mindset is one of 'all problems and challenges are ours'. If all the team members have strong reward links to the team goals, then this should be straightforward. If as in pseudo-teams there is purely individual reward, then this will be more challenging.

3. **Work together to produce an Action Plan for recovery.** Usually when teams hit that 'eureka' moment when they have discovered the root cause of a problem or challenge then producing an action plan is straightforward because the 'eureka' moment produces motivation. It may be that the team has the capabilities to put the action plan in place immediately but it also maybe the case that new capabilities are required to overcome the

challenge. This, then is simply put into the team development plan so that the team can be self-sufficient moving forward when the capabilities are delivered via the development plan.

It is still very much the case that under-performance is attributed to individuals and the expectation is that the team manager deals with this on a one-to-one basis. This is pseudo-team and potential team behaviour and whilst it may still occur at a high-performance team level, the preferred option at high performance level is to have team focused accountability around challenges and to tackle the challenges head on as a team. It may that one individual is still the root cause of the challenge or under performance and ultimately needs the team manager to deal with the situation but taking a team approach to this produces real awareness in individuals and a peer pressure that, if applied positively and constructively, can support individuals to turn their performance around quite markedly.

Team Peer Appraisal – A more Productive Method?

Appraisals, regardless of role and of industry can be challenging processes. In this chapter, I would like to explore two ways forward. Firstly, I will look at the traditional process for appraisal, that being the team manager to team member one to one, and then look at a process I believe more companies with teams should be adopting. This is the team peer appraisal process where the team members appraise each other and that includes an appraisal of the team manager by the team itself. If the team is working together throughout the year, then the members are best placed to appraise their peers than simply leaving it to the team manager to do the traditional 1:1? Whilst the team manager may also be a member of a management team, they could take the team's appraisal feedback to that management team as part of their overall appraisal feedback.

Firstly, let us go back a step and look at the standard, more traditional method of appraisal process for many teams in industry today. This is still the one-to-one team manager:

team member approach. If this is done correctly it can be very productive and motivational, but it depends on several factors.

1. The team manager doing the appraisal must be capable with good appraisal skills, up to date correct information and have no favourites within his or her team.
2. The appraisee must also have good influencing skills and have their appraisal information up to date to present their case for their preferred performance rating.
3. Theoretically, the end of year appraisal should be a "rubber-stamping" exercise and in effect should be a "4th Quarter Review" with no surprises. As the previous three quarterly reviews will have been structured to review business and personal development plans and to monitor and guide the progress of each plan, the final end of year review should hold no surprises what so-ever.

This all sounds straightforward although there are several challenges that both team managers and team members face in getting to a situation where the year-end appraisal is as straightforward and "painless" as it should be.

1. Many team managers do not hold structured quarterly reviews where time is taken to analyse fully the team member's business and development plans. These can be very informal and may not even happen. Many team managers simply do an informal mid-year review and then the final year end with little review and coaching in between these.

2. Many team managers by the time it comes to the year-end appraisal, go into them with their mind made up as to what a particular team member is going to get in terms of a performance or appraisal rating. It is all decided on limited, top-line information and perhaps "gut feel" with this being due to the lack of structure in approach to the review process.

3. On the other hand, in many cases, team members can go into the appraisal with a negative mindset that says, "I'll just have to accept to accept what my manager gives me".

Bad and ineffective appraisals lead to individual de-motivation and ineffective teamwork. So, what should managers be doing to make their one-to-one appraisals more effective and motivational?

a. Make sure they have good, effective appraisal skills.

b. Go into appraisals with an open mind and be prepared to be influenced by facts and figures not by judgements.

c. Ensure that you hold regular reviews where you are guiding and coaching team members towards their "appraisal aims". The benefit of this is that the manager will know whether the team member is "on track" at any given point during the year. Quarterly reviews are regular enough without being too frequent. Anything less frequent, I would suggest is unacceptable.

If a team manager follows these steps then the year-end appraisal is very much a "rubber stamping" exercise and can be used to start the planning for the following year, rather than just concentrating on the year just passed.

Rather than continue with the established team manager to team member 1:1 appraisal, many high-performance teams have introduced a process whereby the team members do the appraisals as a team. This involves the team manager playing a coaching and facilitator role with the team and allowing the team members to decide what each team member receives as a performance rating at the year end.

I have suggested this approach on many occasions, and this has been met with cynicism and disbelief. The reasons for this cynicism as regards team peer appraisal (as per manager feedback) are as follows:

a. "Not enough time to train the team members in how to perform peer appraisal."

b. "No internal expertise to ensure good skills uptake and to facilitate such peer meetings"

c. "It's quicker and less stressful just to tell them what they are getting".

d. "The team manager is "scared" of giving up control, either in terms of how they might look to their senior managers or in terms of their belief in the ability of their team members to give themselves "honest" appraisal ratings".

e. "It's change – and not the way we do things round here!"

However, many team managers I have interviewed can also see the benefits:

a. "Done well, I can see a lot of honesty coming out. I know that there is discontent when some team members appear to get a better appraisal rating than perhaps, they should get"

b. "It would help the team members grow as a result of the fairness and honesty. It would also help the trust levels between team members and managers"

c. "We would probably get a better picture of reality in terms of recognising true performance."

d. "I believe that the skills of the team member and managers would increase as a result"

e. "Although I am wary of how best we could do this, I see that it could free up a lot my time so that I could work on more strategic priorities"

There are numerous advantages to going down the route of team peer appraisal, but it can be challenging, and it does not happen overnight!

The benefits are:

- Encourages mutual support and challenge.
- Enables further cohesion of team 'bonds' and 'spirit'.
- Keeps team and individual performance on track to success.
- Enables managers to focus on more strategic imperatives by freeing up time.
- Prevents management 'bias'.
- Provides sustainable individual competency development and a 'growth' mindset.

There are some essential skills and mindsets needed for it to happen productively.

1. Team managers need to have the mindset that says, "My team is composed of mature, capable adults who given time, support and the right skills, will make this initiative work" If you do not have this

mindset as a manager do not attempt this – in fact if you do not have this mindset then, I my opinion, you should not be managing full stop!

2. Team managers should be leading the way and in their own specific management team, be going through the process first. Team managers must also be open to being appraised by the very people they manage.

3. Team managers must have the skills to ensure the process works. The main skills are that of giving and receiving feedback, coaching and of group facilitation. These are the three skills which, in my experience, managers need to work a lot on. They are difficult skills to grasp but well worth the time and effort.

4. Communication must be of the highest order. People must know what is happening, why it is happening and what the various steps are that will enable it to happen. As in any selling situation, the benefits to every individual must be clearly spelt out and each manager should take time with each individual to make sure they fully understand what is happening and what the benefits are to the individual.

5. Planning skills must also be good. In the early days, time must be built in so that training and trial runs take place. In today's high-pressure industry with the need for results paramount, spending time on any form of development sometimes becomes an after-thought.

There are six key steps that should be considered when implementing a team peer appraisal process:

- Check that the process is appropriate for the team in that the team members work closely together and as such can give constructive feedback on work performance.
- Design a robust process that everyone understands.
- Ensure senior leadership 'buy-in' and ongoing support.
- Communicate the specific reasons for the process being implemented and the specific benefits that the organisation, the teams, and the individual team members will gain from it.
- Ensure full individual understanding of the benefits and the steps in the process.
- Build in a review process and a communications strategy that informs stakeholders of progress and results.

If you are a team member then there are some key things you need to embrace and remember:

- Make sure you have a full understanding of the process and the benefits to both the team and you, as an individual.
- Enter the process with an open and honest mindset.
- Be prepared to support and challenge your peers constructively.
- Be up front and open about your own level of performance – highlight where you are on track and do not be afraid to highlight where you are behind and where perhaps you are struggling.
- Be open to feedback, suggestions, advice, and ideas.

All in all, my experience of supporting the implementation of such a team peer appraisal scheme (and also of taking part) is that it can be fraught with emotion and negativity to begin with, but with perseverance and patience, when implemented well, it is definitely the way forward for those teams whose individual team members work closely together. Provided the team managers are supportive, capable of leading the way by demonstrating the skills, and not afraid to trust their teams, then team peer appraisal can work, and work incredibly well. But make no mistake – it is challenging in the short term, but it is a key aspect of high-performance teams.

12

Team Reward
& Recognition

As we discussed earlier in this book, reward and recognition is vital if individuals are to remain motivated and productive. The same goes for teams but how can you reward a team of people so that each and every team member is continually motivated?

Teams overall are not motivated by "blanket" schemes such as cash bonuses or holidays. Such schemes particularly where money has to be divided up based on contribution and/ or success can be downright destructive if mis-handled. And do all team members want to go on that super four-day trip to Dubai?

If, you as a team manager are going to reward and recognise your team for their efforts and success why not consider the following:

- Make the next team meeting a good one at a good venue such as a top-class hotel with leisure facilities. Throw is some leisure time such as a round of golf or a massage if company policy allows this.

- Get the team members involved in the formation and running of the meeting so that it is their meeting, with the manager having only a "slot". Shared leadership is a powerful motivator as we have discussed several times in earlier chapters.
- Run some simple competitions whereby the team votes for individuals within the team. e.g., "Most Improved Performer"
- Run a team newsletter or e-newsletter, where successes are listed and perhaps individuals interviewed on specific project work.
- Give the team a slice of your budget to work with in relation to project work or setting up the motivational team meeting.
- Use some of your budget to perhaps upgrade equipment such as the latest laptop, mobile phone, car, or essential work equipment.
- How about a free lunch or dinner for them and their spouses? Concert tickets?
- Talk to them! As a team tell them how much you value their expertise and effort. Tell them as a team and as individuals!

These are just some simple things you can do to thank and motivate a team as a whole but it is not as plain sailing as this. Sometimes there will be distinct differences in performance on a team objective or project and to ensure that everyone is rewarded according to their performance the team manager will have to ensure that they oversee reward schemes that make sure that performance is taken into account, especially where money is at stake!

If you are considering a reward scheme that involves bonus money, then how do you go about ensuring a fair distribution of that money based on performance? And who makes the decisions? You as the manager? Or do you let the team decide? Consider the following before proceeding:

- The scheme must be simple to understand and simple to monitor and calculate. Avoid complicated schemes that need a Masters in Astrophysics to decipher!
- Everyone must fully understand what he or she needs to do to make the scheme work for him or her.
- Updates must be regular and a mechanism for queries must be put in place.

Rewarding a team of individuals can be challenging given the different styles, personalities and needs involved but with a little dedicated time and input from the team, good reward schemes and initiatives can be produced which will help to ensure that the team gets the recognition they deserve.

13

Mistakes to Avoid as a Team Manager or Team Leader

I do not normally focus on the negative but over the years I have found that if you point out the potential hazards or mistakes that should be avoided many team managers and team leaders actually pay more attention to these than if you actually point out the positive things they should be doing! So, if you are a team manager or team leader then make sure you avoid the following mistakes when looking to lead your team to high performance and the results you desire.

The mistakes are easy to make (believe me I have made a few!) but they are all easy to either prevent or rectify.

1. When starting out with a new team **do not 'fly into task'!** It is tempting to get cracking straight away and launch into the various tasks that the team have been designated to perform. Stop, think, and get the team together to work on the essential basics that underpin teamwork such as purpose, specific aims, goals and objectives, roles,

development plans, team member strengths, needs, expectations, rewards, review and decision-making processes and stakeholder management. Remember the PARTNERS™ process. There is a lot to cover before you even start to fly into task and if you do not stop and work on the basics then chaos and confusion will potentially reign! Remember the 'storming' phase of team development is not a great place for the team to get stuck!

2. **Do not sit back and expect the team alone to work on the basics.** I encountered a manager who once attempted to start the team off with some of the essential basics but left the room to allow the team to work on these team basics with the instruction that they wanted a full report when they returned! Not a great start for this team! As a team manager get involved, lead from the front but take an active and equal role when working on the basics. Everyone in the team should all be in this together and especially when you are putting your team contract and development plan together.

3. **Do not be overly 'dictatorial'** and take over the start-up team meeting or any team meeting for that matter. Whilst the team may need direction on certain aspects of what lies ahead, it is always best to balance the direction with a degree of coaching and facilitation. Good team leadership is a balance of appropriate direction and selective coaching.

4. Get into the way of communicating about **'our team'** as opposed to 'my team'. After all you do

not own the team, do you? If you want to build inclusivity, then when the team members hear you talking about 'our team' it does really help to build trust. Remember the ICA and Diamond-Motivation™ models.

5. **Do not shirk away from being 'vulnerable'!** Being 'vulnerable' is simply about being 'open' and owning up to your weaknesses and your mistakes. It is a real strength for a manager to be able to do this and again shows the team that you are 'human' with the result that it brings trust and support. Be prepared to openly share your responsibilities and objectives with the team and be upfront about the ones you are capable and comfortable with, but also those you are going to find challenging. Being open about this also builds trust and increased support.

6. **Avoid the 'blame game'.** Too many managers are quick to 'point the finger' and look for 'scapegoats'. This can totally destroy team trust and cohesion and should be avoided at all costs. When things go wrong – stop – take a breather – and then start to seek to understand what may have gone wrong and get to the 'root cause'. Be inquisitive, investigative and solutions orientated, but do not play the 'blame game'. It is weak leadership; in fact, it is not even leadership of any description!

7. Do not allocate roles and responsibilities without understanding your **team members' strengths and weaknesses.** This is a common mistake, and you should play to the team's strengths. If

someone in the team has specific weaknesses that are needing developed as they need those skills for their role then ensure a development plan to build their capability, otherwise get people working on projects where their skills and motivations sit nicely. If you are the type of manager that allocates tasks to people you know will struggle at the task to show them up, then get out of management! Make sure you do some 'strengths profiling' of your team.

8. **Make sure you praise and praise often!** It is not difficult to say 'thank you' where and when it is deserved so make sure you do it. Simple praise is one of the biggest (if not the biggest) motivators that you can use. The other great motivator is to be an active listener to ensure you do a lot of listening. Also make sure you celebrate the small successes as well as the big ones!

9. Do not go long periods of time without a **review of progress**! It is vital that time is put in to review the team's progress and not just the team business plan. Along with reviewing the development plan make sure that the 'team contract' and the agreements within the contract are being implemented and demonstrated effectively. Ensure your review sessions are inclusive, motivational, and productive and include stakeholders where possible to get an 'outsider' view and input.

10. **Do not let stress get the better of you!** I have seen too many managers (and I have also suffered from this on occasion) take on too much with the

result that the stress builds up and effects them both mentally and physically. Make sure you look after yourself and have coping strategies. Keep yourself fit, watch your diet, and look to manage your workload by saying 'no' where appropriate. If you have the trust and support of your senior manager as well as support from the team then this will go a long way to allow you to manage the stress accordingly. If you do not have this support, then it can be downward spiral for both you and the team.

14

Company Culture and 'Psychological Safety'

Throughout this book we have discussed what it takes to build a team from being a pseudo team through to a high-performance team and in many ways, we have focused at lot on specifically what the team must do in order to go through the various stages of team development. We have not touched on a couple of key areas that have been (and are still being) discussed at length by various consultancies and academic institutions as we move through the COVID-19 pandemic. These are the impact of the company culture on both teams and individuals and the need to ensure that within any company culture there must be a real emphasis on providing what is being called, 'psychological safety'.

Let me start with 'psychological safety'. There are various definitions of 'psychological safety', but they all amount to the same thing. Psychological safety is being able to be one's self without fear of negative consequences of self-image, status, or career. It means that team members should have the ability within any company culture to feel 'safe' and to be able to outline exactly what their ideas, hopes, fears and concerns are without having any source of fear that will prevent them from doing so. In high performance teams there is an environment and culture created that allows the team members to speak freely and thus ensure that key aspects of motivation (as discussed earlier via ICA, Maslow's, and Diamond-Motivation™) are in place. This takes great team leadership, a 'live' team contract which sustains team member accountability, and a great stakeholder management plan to ensure that this team culture remains buoyant and powerful. Above all if the team is a true high performing team then the results will 'speak for themselves' and the high-performance team can then influence and perhaps 'shape' the company culture moving forward. This all depends, though, on the quality and calibre of the senior leadership within the organisation and unfortunately, a 'weak', 'ego-centric' and 'command and control' centred leadership can severely dent the progress of high-performance teams as well as potentially impact negatively on a positive culture of empowerment and psychological safety across the organisation.

If the company does have a culture that is not authentically team focused then it can be challenging for high-performance teams, particularly those who have gained high-performance by pursuing their own 'path'. I have experienced teams, who have gone against (or adapted when not supposed to) a company strategy (and they have been successful) who have 'lost' their manager due to going against the strategy. The company put 'spin' on the team's results by saying that the performance was the result of good individual performance and 'favourable' market conditions but in many ways, they could have had even greater results if they had a more effective team manager who had kept to the company strategy! Employee turnover increased after that episode funnily enough! Unfortunately, in 'top down' company cultures where a 'one size fits all approach' is favoured and deviation from any strategy is frowned upon, many team managers and teams can find themselves in a 'Catch-22' situation. If the team agrees that their own strategy is right for their business (and clients) and goes ahead and delivers top class results, then do they stand up for themselves and say – 'We did it our way and look at the results'? Or do they sit back and let the company think that the results were due to delivering the company strategy? If they stand up for themselves, they could be (or the manager could be) 'scapegoated' with the same result of the previous example in that they do not get the full recognition for their success (or even worse). If they remain quiet and simply let the company think they got the results the 'company way' then no change will happen, and the company will simply reinforce its stance that their overall strategy is sacrosanct and indeed effective. The high performing team, in this scenario, continues to operate but their 'psychological safety' is compromised which will inevitably lead to a decrease in performance though time and an increase in team membership turnover.

So, if companies are truly authentic and they do want to ensure 'psychological safety' for all their employees they must ensure that this goes beyond a 'tick-box' approach of simply supplying 'wellbeing' and 'resilience' workshops and webinars. Training and developing team managers in such disciplines is also good (and this can be further enhanced through the team development strategies advised within this book), but the overall company culture must be one of openness, honesty, innovation, creativity, and empowerment and authentically 'living' and 'breathing' the key values that underpin these. If you are to ensure high-performance teams are created and sustained, then the organisation must fully support the development of teams and teamwork. Senior leadership then must 'walk the talk' and positively encourage, embrace, and look forward to the increasing level of 'positive' challenge that high performance teams can bring to senior leadership.

To summarise:

- 'Psychological safety' starts from the top and goes beyond the company simply providing 'wellbeing' and 'resilience' workshops and manager training in these areas. These can help, but senior leadership must be authentic in all they do and lead the way in creating a culture that is not solely 'top down' and is empowering, allowing entrepreneurship, creativity, and innovation to take place. It is about allowing teams to do the right things for both clients and the company. The results will follow.

- Teams can provide their own 'psychological safety' by having the essential conversations around the creation of the team contract and by having great team leadership through the team manager or leader. Teams can create their own self-directed culture and lead from the 'bottom up' through great performance, being courageous and having a dynamic stakeholder action plan. True high-performance teams lead by example and actively 'manage up the way' so that they can influence overall company culture.

15

Consider Recruiting a Team Champion

Many team managers are under intense pressure. I recently read a report by the Gartner organisation that stated that '58% of sales managers struggle to complete all assigned tasks, these managers may be now managing teams that are even more remote than they have been previously, and the teams may be larger with more members which brings on even more time and pressure challenges. Add in the constant pressure on the delivery of outputs and a possible lack of resources available to develop the team, this will no doubt contribute to the additional workload that can affect the manager's ability to focus on effective teamwork. It is also likely that the team manager has not been trained in effective teamwork as many leadership courses are 'light' on the teamwork aspect. In addition, it may also be that the team manager's role may have increasing project and customer work that takes them away from the actual team. You can then have a situation where the team could be left to 'fend for themselves' in many aspects.

As we have already discussed earlier in this book, a good team manager will delegate appropriate tasks and projects and make sure these projects fit with the strengths of the individual team members, making sure that they do not conflict with their key individual roles and responsibilities. The good team manager may also ensure that team members work together on projects where appropriate so 'teamwork within the team' is encouraged. One particularly important delegated role that has worked well in some teams is that of the **'team development champion'**. This would be a role which would work with the team manager to ensure that all elements of team development are a priority and are developed so that the team is operating at their maximum effectiveness and at a high-performance level. There are several key advantages to this role being created:

1. It keeps team development and performance on the team's agenda.
2. It allows the manager to ensure balance between their own key responsibilities.
3. It allows the manager to develop their own coaching and mentoring skills.
4. The 'team champion' can grow and develop skills in the areas of team development, coaching, training, and facilitation and as such can be an important 'stepping-stone' towards team manager positions.
5. There is a 'team development' peer voice within the team.
6. Team development towards high team performance can be achieved quicker.

As in any delegated task situation the amount of time a team champion can spend in this specific development task should be agreed and contracted. I have experienced new team champions take on the role with great enthusiasm and let their key and core responsibilities suffer as a result, so great care must be taken to ensure the correct balance.

The other key area that needs to be addressed is that the 'team champion' will need to be trained effectively in the key aspects of team development because it is almost certain that the 'team champion's' line manager will not have the time to do this, and probably not have the experience or expertise in order to coach and mentor the champion in all essential aspects of team development. This training should be taken on via the company's L&D or Training Team and in the absence of such a dedicated resource, then external support should be sought.

The key areas of a team that the champion will need to be trained will include:

- Definitions and Types of Team and their place on the team performance curve.
- The Key Stages of Team Development from Forming through to Performing.
- Accelerator (or Kick-Start) processes such as PARTNERS™ to embed the team basics such as purpose, goal setting, contracting and stakeholder management.
- Personality and Strengths profiles of team members to ensure clarity and understanding of behavioural style preferences and where people will be best placed for projects.
- Team Decision Making and Problem-Solving techniques.
- Effective Team Meetings and Review processes.
- How to manage conflict within the team.
- Reward and Recognition processes that keep motivation, focus and performance high.

All in all, the focus on any development should be on ensuring the basics of team development are learned and embedded and an action plan should be agreed with the team champion's line manager. In this respect this must be a real partnership with the line manager supporting the team champion in a coaching capacity. This is most definitely not a situation for a team manager to abdicate responsibility and if the team manager is not comfortable supporting the team champion then they need to gain support from their L&D Department.

With the challenge of ensuring that team development is kept to the forefront of an organisation's capability plan (and especially if 'teamwork' is a key value!) the creation of a 'team champion' for every team that aspires to high performance is one strategy that an organisation should strongly consider.

Your Action Plan

You have come to the end of 'Team Champion'. I would like to summarise what we have covered, in the form of an action plan which you can take and use as a framework for getting your new team off to the best possible start or if you are leading an existing team, put steps in place to ensure increased performance.

Get your team together either virtually or physically, and ensure that you put in place the following:

1. Agree the **Purpose** of your team. What is the team's reason for being? What is the team providing and for whom?

2. Agree the specific **Aims, Goals, Targets or Objectives** that the team must achieve. Check full clarity and understanding with everyone as to what the team must achieve. Make sure the aims, goals, targets, or objectives are **SMART.**

3. You now have the basics of a **Team Contract or Charter** and this can be completed later when

adding in the agreed behaviours, review processes and stakeholder plan if so desired. A Contract or Charter can embrace all the aspects of the PARTNERS™ process but the very minimum I would suggest is that it covers the Purpose, Aims & Goals, Agreed Behaviours, and the agreed Review process.

4. Agree the specific **Roles and Responsibilities** of each team member and ensure these will achieve the aims, goals, targets, or objectives and in turn satisfy the team's purpose. Make sure these are shared and understood by all members of the team including the team manager or team leader.

5. Discuss with the team what skills and capabilities are required to achieve the team's Aims, Goals, Targets or Objectives. Create a **Team Development Plan** which covers key capability or knowledge areas that every member of the team must develop. In the case of only a few members requiring upskilling and / or knowledge enhancement then build this into their individual development plans.

6. Consider doing a full team **Behavioural Styles Exercise** alongside completing **Strengths Profiling** for the team. These are useful exercises to raise awareness of individual's style preferences and behaviours as well as identify who is placed for what projects. They are fun exercises to do as well and tend to bring the team 'closer' together in terms of awareness, rapport, and appreciation.

7. Ensure you carry out the **'Needs and Expectations'** exercise which will allow every team member to express what they need (in terms of demonstrated behaviours) from working

in the team. It is also vital that all expectations are managed so ensure the team manager or leader expresses what they expect from the team and do similar with what the team members expect from line management or the team leader. It's also important under the 'expectations' heading that everyone knows how **Decisions** will be made by the team. What decisions will be made by the team manager alone? By the team? By individuals?

8. Make sure the agreed behaviours are documented in the **Team Charter** and discuss and agree how 'divergence' from the agreements in the charter are to be handled. What if a team member's behaviour is that which is the opposite of what has been agreed in the charter? How will the team deal with this?

9. Agree a **Review process** where both the Team's Business (or Account or Projects) Plan is reviewed and, also, include a review of the Team Development Plan. The review process should include both performance and development.

10. It is important that team discuss and have full clarity on company **Reward and Recognition** schemes. How can the team maximise these? Also, what reward and recognition processes or schemes can the team put in place for themselves – the company schemes?

11. To ensure full support for the team from senior managers it is important to agree who the key 'stakeholders' are in the company who are influenced by the actions of the team or are dependent on the team. Build a **Stakeholder Map** and then devise a plan as to how the team can enlist the support of these key individuals. This

is important regardless of company culture and is essential if the company culture is not one which is totally convinced by the powerful impact of teams.

12. Consider appointing and training a **team development champion** to assist in the team's development. It does not always have to be the sole responsibility of the team manager to put processes in place to enable the team's development to high-performance.

Below is an example of a Team 'Readiness' Checker which covers the key points above and which you can use to ensure that you and your team are 'ready' for your journey to high performance. You can get copies of this plus examples of the team contract and team development plan by emailing me at allan@partnersteamdevelopment.com

Best of luck with your journey to high performance!

Table 3 – The PARTNERS™ Team Readiness Checker

PARTNERS™ Team Readiness Checker

Team Basic Essentials	Questions to Consider	No	Maybe	Yes	Actions to get to Yes	By Whom?	By When?
Purpose (Vision if full company 'team' approach)	Has the team worked on, agreed and fully understand the purpose / vision of the team?			Yes			
Aims, Goals & Specific Objectives	Have the team agreed and fully understand the specific aims, goals and objectives that the team have to achieve?			Yes			
Roles & Responsibilities	Do all team members fully understand their roles and responsibilities?		Maybe		Revisit understanding of roles at the next team meeting	Team	09-Oct
	Has everyone in the team shared their role responsibilities and individual objectives?	No			Make sure objectives are shared across the whole team. By email prior to next meeting	Team	02-Oct
Training Needs	Have the overall team training / capability needs been identified?		Maybe		Revisit with help of the training department	Team leader with Training	30-Sep
	Is there a specific training plan in place for the team?	No			Revisit with help of the training department	Team leader with Training	30-Sep
Needs of the Team Members	Has there been an open and honest discussion around the personal needs of the individual team members in terms of working in the team?	No			Make sure this happens with external facilitator support - discuss with training department	Team Leader with Training	30-Sep
Expectations	Has there been an open and honest discussion between team manager / leader and the team members as to what is expected from everyone?	No			Make sure this happens with external facilitator support - discuss with training department	Team Leader with Training	30-Sep
Review & Recognition	Has a specific review process been agreed along with a timetable?			Yes			
	Is there a company reward scheme that rewards and recognises the achievements of the team?			Yes			
	Do all the Team Members fully understand the Company Scheme?		Maybe		Send out scheme again and ensure all team members revisit this. Hold Skype to revisit	Team Reward Champion	16-Sep
	Have the team discussed their own internal reward and recognition scheme and created their own scheme?	No			Begin discussions on Skype - ideas to be generated prior to the Skype	Team Reward Champion	09-Sep
Stakeholders	Has the team identified their key stakeholders and put a plan in place to ensure all stakeholders are managed constructively so that the team and the stakeholders benefit?	No			Ensure slot on the agenda of next meeting to work on stakeholder map and action plan	Team Leader	09-Oct
Contract / Charter / Agreement	Has a team agreement/ charter / contract been created summarising agreements made above?	No			Create small team project group to work on this and present back to team when complete.	TM1 / TM2 / TM3	30-Nov

Bibliography

I would like to acknowledge the authors of the following books whose writings have given me many ideas and inspiration during my coaching and management career thus far. This list is also intended to serve as a recommended reading list for anyone interested in learning more about team performance, management, and coaching.

Bateman, Trudy & Linley, Alex (2018) *The Strengths Profile Book* Capp Press

Belbin, Meredith R, (1981). *Management Teams – Why they Succeed or Fail* Butterworth Heinemann

Blanchard, Ken, (1994). *The One-Minute Manager Builds High Performing Teams*. Harper Collins

Craven, Caspar. (2020). *Be More Human*. Amazon Books

Katzenbach, Jon R & Smith, Douglas K (1993) *The Wisdom of Teams*. Harvard Business School Press

Kerr, James (2013) *Legacy – 15 Lessons in Leadership* Constable & Robinson

Landsberg, Max, (1996). *The Tao of Coaching*. Harper Collins

Lencioni, Patrick (2005) *Overcoming the Five Dysfunctions of a Team* Jossey Bass

Lillibridge, E. Michael (1998). *The People Map*. Lilmat Press

Mackintosh, Allan M (2003) *The Successful Coaching Manager* Matador

Mulligan, John, (1988). *The Personal Management Handbook*. Warner Books

Murphy, Martin (2019) *From Mercenaries to Missionaries*. Rethink Press

Phillips, Nicola (1995). *Motivating for Change*. Pitman Publishing

Robbins, Harvey & Finley Michael, (1995) *Why Teams Don't Work* Pacesetter Books

Robbins, Harvey & Finley Michael, (2000) *The New Why Teams Don't Work* Pacesetter Books – Berrett-Koehler

Whitmore, John, (1992). *Coaching for Performance*. Nicholas Brealey

Wilson Learning, (2011) *The Social Styles Handbook*, Nova Vista

About the Author

Allan Mackintosh has been in business since 1982 and has worked with corporate teams and professional sports teams during this time, both as a full-time employee and as an external self-employed consultant and coach. Whilst most of his working life has been spent in roles associated with sales, sales management, management training and team coaching within the UK and Ireland pharmaceutical industry, a period of self-employed consultancy between 2001 and 2009, saw him work with many other industries including Finance, Aerospace, Engineering, Professional Sports, Distribution, Logistics, and the NHS amongst others. After a further eleven years in pharmaceuticals, he is now, once again, running his own consultancy, Partners Team Development, a consultancy focused on enabling corporate teams at all levels to achieve high performance.

An accomplished author of articles, he published his first

book, *The Successful Coaching Manager* (Matador) in 2003 and he is also an accomplished and popular conference speaker having spoken at numerous international pharmaceutical and healthcare conferences across the UK, Europe, and India. Allan is also the creator of innovative team development & coaching models such as Diamond-Motivation™, OUTCOMES™, and PARTNERS™.

 **Matador**

For exclusive discounts on Matador titles,
sign up to our occasional newsletter at
troubador.co.uk/bookshop